Case Studies About Children and Adolescents with Special Needs

Nancy Halmhuber
Eastern Michigan University

Kathleen Jeakle Beauvais
Eastern Michigan University

Allyn and Bacon

Boston • London • Toronto • Sydney • Tokyo • Singapore

To Gary, my husband and best friend

NH

* * * * * *

To my Daddy, the love and light of my life

KJB

Executive Editor: Virginia Lanigan
Editorial Assistant: Erin Liedel
Editorial-Production Administrator: Beth Houston
Editorial-Production Service: Walsh & Associates, Inc.
Composition Buyer: Linda Cox
Manufacturing Buyer: Julie McNeill
Cover Administrator: Linda Knowles

Copyright © 2002 by Allyn & Bacon
A Pearson Education Company
75 Arlington Street
Boston, MA 02116

Internet: www.ablongman.com

ISBN: 0-205-34400-3

Printed in the United States of America
10 9   05

CONTENTS

PREFACE

Five years ago we began team-teaching an introductory course about students with exceptionalities. What is somewhat unique about this partnership is that we represent two separate departments within our college—we are professors of special education (Nancy) and teacher education (Kathleen). We are committed to effective inclusion and the importance of collaboration between special and general educators, believing that these are essential factors to the school success of all students. We attempt to model such collaboration in our team-teaching and approach the content in our course from both special education and general education perspectives.

In this team-taught course were students preparing to be special educators, general educators, physical education teachers, art teachers, music teachers, speech-language pathologists, and early childhood specialists. We discovered the students were as varied as their majors. While some students were talking about their grandchildren, others were living away from home for the first time. Some people had extensive experience with students with disabilities; others expressed their fear and concern about having these students in their future classrooms. The challenge was to establish a shared experience and frame of reference that would facilitate discussion and understanding about educating children with disabilities among the university students.

After teaching together for a few semesters we realized that we needed some additional course materials that engaged our students in the practical application of the principles and realities of inclusion. We reviewed the available compilations of case studies and, although they were interesting and well written, we found each lacking in one specific area. They presented each case independently, unrelated in any way to other cases in the volume. In our opinion, this did not reflect the reality of inclusion. Although each student's needs are unique to that individual, they are not unrelated to each other. Students with special needs are often in the same classroom, certainly within the same schools and district. We wanted a set of case studies that reflected that reality, a set of case studies where the students, teachers, administrators and resource people did not disappear at the conclusion of each case. Our solution was to develop this set of integrated case studies that could be used to foster creative discussion; we created the Dewey Consolidated School District (DCSD) within the Bell Regional Educational Services Agency (BRESA).

In our university class, we use the case studies as a group activity to supplement the textbook and lecture information. Our students are divided into teams and the teams remain intact throughout the semester. We provide our students some initial training in skills that facilitate successful team experiences and have them practice these skills in a special case that reflects the experience of one of the teams that struggled in our class. We attempt to have at least one special education major and also students representing preschool, elementary, and secondary education majors comprising the rest of the team. The teams usually number between six and eight students. The student teams meet periodically during class time to discuss the issues presented by each case. We believe this format provides a learning experience similar to the process that takes place in schools, where teachers, parents, and various resource people meet and collaborate on a plan for a student. It also provides students a chance to hear information and the opinions of their peers who may have a different perspective. The prospective teachers then have an opportunity to learn how to negotiate and celebrate these differences

There are some other instructional features that we have included in the book that we found helpful as we organized our class. One is the Case Matrix. The Matrix is designed to give a quick overview of the issues we considered as we wrote the cases about the various disability areas. If you want to organize discussion around issues or looking for a specific content field, this would be of assistance. We have also included an opportunity near the beginning of each case for the reader to reflect on what types of information and resources might add to the resolution of the dilemma. There are structured activities and questions at the end of each case that we have used to generate discussion and more reflection.

Whether you assign these cases in a group or as individual assignments, we hope they contribute to your students' learning and understanding about the issues that need to be addressed to insure that all students have the opportunity to reach their potential.

Acknowledgments

We want to acknowledge all those students who reacted to and discussed the various cases as we developed them over a five-year period. In addition to our students, we wish to acknowledge the support we received from the State of Michigan that provided the initial support during the design of these cases. Eastern Michigan University also provided support in the form of an interdisciplinary grant that provided the resources to interview our colleagues about the students in the cases and to check with curriculum experts and school-based personnel about the authenticity of the cases. To all these people we gratefully thank you for your time, knowledge, and encouragement.

We appreciate the support from Allyn and Bacon staff as they guided us through the steps required to see this manuscript in print. We appreciate their patience, expertise, and helpful advice. Reviewers provided us with different perspectives and their insightful comments strengthened the applicability of the cases.

Last, we wish to acknowledge the love and support of our families and friends who have always been there when we needed a nudge or a hug.

	LD	ADHD	SLI	MI/MR	TAG	EI/BD
ASSESSMENT, DEFINITION	IQ/achievement discrepancy	disruptive behaviors	unintelligible speech, language delay	IQ, adaptive skills deficits	unknown	classroom behavior
PEERS	name-calling and friendship	alienated	lack of peer interaction	teasing, social isolation	"silly" and "weird"	disrupted by outbursts, alienated
DEVELOPMENTAL PROGRESS	delayed in reading	motor skills advanced	acquired (stroke)	fetal alcohol syndrome	within normal limits	delays in language arts
GENDER	females	male	female	male	female	female
SOCIOECONOMIC STATUS	low SES; middle class	low SES; accessing services	middle class	retired, blue collar	low SES	blue collar
FAMILY	single parent; nuclear	nuclear	nuclear	grandparent caretakers	nuclear and extended	female, single parent; history of abuse
SERVICE DELIVERY METHOD	inclusion	Head Start	SLI and pre-primary consultants	voc-tech center	options for discussion	resource room
RELATED SERVICES	tutoring	school psychologist, pre-primary consultant	none	none	none	social worker
GRADE LEVEL	elementary	preschool	preschool	high school	elementary	middle school
TEACHER EFFICACY, EXPECTATIONS	concerned about equity and scheduled meetings	called in the school psychologist	increasingly frustrated	concerned about transition to adulthood	puzzled and surprised	needing more successful interventions
TECHNOLOGY	none	none	augmentative communication	none	none	none
CURRICULUM MODIFICATIONS	delivery of lessons, possible team-teaching	to be determined	assessment	community-based instruction	options for discussion	behavioral contract
LEARNING CHARACTERISTICS	average intelligence	inattentive, hyperactive, impulsive	average cognition, fine motor delay	basic skills deficits	exceptional in science	above grade level math skills
SUBJECT AREA, CONTEXT	reading	play	speech and language	voc-tech	science	math

POHI (HEALTH)	HI	VI	AUTISTIC SPECTRUM DISORDER	TBI	MULTIPLY IMPAIRED	IEPT
sickle-cell anemia	bilateral moderate to severe loss	blind; retinopathy of prematurity	social skills and communication	traumatic brain injury	spastic cerebral palsy, TMI	to be determined
relationships interrupted by hospitalizations	communication	first experience with typical students	communication	friendships	modeling appropriate social skills	leader
genetic counseling	other areas of development within normal limits	other developmental skills within normal limits	inconsistent	delays in speech, language, fine and gross motor skills	delays in skill areas	within normal limits
male	female	male	male	female	female	male
upper middle class, military	professional	middle class	middle class, military	middle class, high medical expenses	blue collar	blue collar
male single parent, transient	nuclear, iimportant extended family	nuclear	nuclear	nuclear	female, single parent	nuclear
homebound teacher	HI and SLI consultants	self-contained classroom	resource room	resource room	center-based program	options for discussion
physician	language and deaf culture, hospital audiologist	goal ball		SLI and physical therapy	OT, PT, SLI	educational planning team
elementary	preschool	elementary	middle school	middle school	elementary	high school
frustrated by multiple and extended absences	anxious about inclusion	concerned about injury; open to learning	hopeful, committed to accommodations	not properly informed and oriented	unknown	concerned
video	fm system and hearing aids	vision braille	computer	electronic note taker	adaptive writing tool	none
cooperative group project	language enrichment and visual cues	goal ball and tactile stimulus	e-mail	needed and addressed	specialized curriculum	modifications needed
absenteeism	oral vs. manual approach	bright, capable, self-sufficient	poor motor skills	irregular speech, delayed processing	developmental delays	below average in writing ability
social studies	language development	physical education	language arts	music	general	academic classes

1 Dewey Consolidated School District

Bell Regional Educational Services Agency (BRESA) is a fictional regional edu-cational agency that is part of the state administrative structure for providing edu-cation to all children within the state. These regional agencies are directly responsible to the State Board of Education for implementation of policies and pro-cedures in their constituent local school districts. They also provide a variety of support services in general, special, and vocational educational programs that local school districts may not be able to provide due to funding limitations. These services in the area of special education may include monitoring implementation of IDEA-97, consulting in low incidence areas (visually impaired, hearing impaired), providing direct student programming in more restrictive environments (center-based programs), and ancillary services such as physical therapy or occu-pational therapy. Within the umbrella of BRESA are fourteen different school dis-tricts. These districts include suburban districts, an urban district and the Dewey Consolidated School District (DCSD). Depending on the needs of students within each local district, the demand for services from BRESA varies. For the DCSD, BRESA provides teacher consultant services, preschool special education pro-gramming, ancillary services personnel, vocational center, technology assistance, and assists in monitoring the implementation of IDEA-97.

The DCSD Annual Report follows closely the format of an annual report, which, in some states, each local district is required to make available to citizens and organizations within the community. It represents a narrative layman's approach rather than the more typical statistical state report.

District Information and Annual Report

The Dewey Consolidated School District Annual Report is a continuation of the yearly report series, which was begun in 1982. This report is also written in com-pliance with Public Act 25 of 1990 that requires that such reports be made avail-able annually to school district residents. It is hoped that through these reports residents will be made more aware of their school district's achievements, objectives, and plans for the future.

District Profile

The Dewey Consolidated School District (DCSD) has historical roots that extend back into the 19th century, but its modern history began in 1962 when three local districts (Binet Lake, Lehtinen Township, and Kirk) combined to form the Consolidated District; the elementary, middle school, and high school buildings are located in Lehtinen Township near the Binet Lake boundary. DCSD is one of several constituent districts of Bell Regional Educational Support Agency (BRESA). Dewey Consolidated School District continues to grow in the number of students enrolled, but the communities have retained their individual identities. Brief overviews of the communities are presented below.

Binet Lake represents the smallest of the communities in the district. The housing values in Binet Lake have continued to escalate because of the desirable lakefront property, making them the most expensive in the district. The Binet Lake Hospital is a full-service hospital and offers inpatient, outpatient surgical, and emergency room services. The residents of Binet Lake are likely to have college degrees and are employed by the hospital, work in the professions, or hold upper level management positions. Many of the families are two-income families; there are an average of 1.75 children per family. Most of the children of Binet Lake ride the bus to the consolidated elementary school. The families in Binet Lake expect their children to attend college upon completion of high school. Binet is comprised of 95 percent European American families who attend a variety of local churches and synagogues. There is one private parochial elementary school in Binet Lake.

Lehtinen Township is essentially a rural community. It consists of large tracts of farmland. The families tend to be larger (average children per family is 3.82) than in Binet Lake, and 95 percent of the families who own farms are European Americans. Seasonal farm workers who are Hispanic and Native American tend to live in the surrounding areas, mainly Kirk. The farms tend to be either large and successful, or extremely small, barely providing sufficient income to support the family. Most of the children have chores that need to be completed before and after school.

Transportation is a major concern of these families, because of the distances many of the children have to travel to attend school. A recent trend indicates that many of the middle and upper middle class families of Kirk are moving out to Lehtinen Township. Transportation costs will likely continue to rise.

There is a charter school in Lehtinen Township that is designed for elementary students with an ecological emphasis. Charter schools provide an alternative public educational experience for students, around a specific theme. They are funded by tax dollars and authorized by a traditional educational agency.

Kirk is the most diverse of the three communities. Kirk includes a small army base that is half the size it was ten years ago and an industrial zone, including various tool and die shops that supply parts to the military as well as the state's automotive industries. In addition to the factories, residents of Kirk work in Binet Lake (tourism and hospital) and some have seasonal employment on the larger farms in Lehtinen Township. Over the past ten years, the industrial economic base of Kirk has declined and the unemployment rate has increased. On the average, the residents of Kirk have fewer economic resources than in the neighboring communities. Housing opportunities in Kirk include single-family homes, military base housing, apartments, two low-income housing projects, and one trailer park. The population of Kirk is approximately 50 percent European American, 25 percent Hispanic American, 20 percent African American and 5 percent various other racial ethnic groups (Native American is the largest).

Dewey Consolidated School District has an enrollment of 2,000 students. Projections of future enrollment patterns indicate that Dewey Consolidated School District will continue to grow slowly over the next few years. The growth appears to be centered in Lehtinen Township, where farmland is gradually being developed. It is also anticipated that the enrollment from Kirk may decline as people move out to the Township. If, as rumored, the military base closes next year, this will result in an enrollment drop. Currently the district includes two elementary schools, one middle school, one high school, a preschool special education program, and a community education center sponsored by the Bell Regional Educational Services Agency (BRESA), a garage, an instructional media center, and a central office administration building. The staff at Dewey Consolidated School District—including faculty, administrators, clerical personnel, maintenance personnel, custodians, bus drivers, cafeteria workers, paraprofessionals, and aides—is predominantly white and lives within the district. Although an affirmative action program undertaken by the district has resulted in the recent hiring of several African and Hispanic Americans, the number of minority employees remains disproportionately low as compared to the population.

Dewey Consolidated High School (DCHS)

The DCHS Waves boys' football team won the state football championship this year, beating archrival Mann High School. The DCHS Waves girls' gymnastic team took second in the state gymnastics meet. Other teams that won league or district honors include girls' soccer, boys' golf, marching band, and debate.

The school emphasizes a college prep curriculum that has recently been aligned with the State Wide Assessment Tests (SWAT). This is the statewide test that sets minimum academic standards for students and is used in part to determine school funding and accreditation. Courses include core courses in English grammar, literature (American, English, and World), History (American, World, and European), mathematics (pre-algebra, calculus, geometry, business math, and basic skills), science (biology, chemistry, physics, physical science, and advanced sciences in conjunction with the local community college), economics, speech, American government, and computer literacy. Available electives include Spanish (three years), music (band, orchestra, vocal), industrial education, art, and advanced computer skills (including desk top publishing). Career and technical education is available through the BRESA. The high school employs two counselors. Additionally, some team-taught courses and some AP courses are available. A cooperative arrangement with the Community College permits some seniors to receive college credit as part of their high school day. Some students are on reduced schedules and a "Success Room" is available. The Success Room in a nonspecial education support service where students spend an hour each day working on affective and academic concerns.

Dewey Consolidated Middle School (DCMS)
The Dewey Consolidated Middle School building houses students in grades 6, 7, and 8. The students are grouped in homeroom and receive core academic subjects in homeroom blocks. For example, the sixth grade has six homerooms. The students in each homeroom class remain together and have the same teacher for English and Social Studies, then the entire class moves to the next block with a different teacher for Math and Science. The remaining school hours are for electives, which change every eight weeks. Electives include art, music, gym, computer literacy, life skills, and study hall. Additional supports include team teaching, after-school study/tutoring, and Language Arts Enrichment. Students in the seventh and eighth grade take Reading, Mathematics, Science, and Social Studies SWAT tests. Two tests are taken at each grade level. In addition to the academic program, DCMS White Caps has an intramural sports program, student council, and several in-school recreational programs (including afternoon dances, and evening recreation activities). An activity bus leaves the school about one hour after normal dismissal, and for a nominal fee students can take this bus home.

Dewey Consolidated Elementary School (DCES)
The Dewey Consolidated Elementary School (DCES) houses students K–5. Most students are bussed to and from school. For the latchkey program, which provides after school supervision, parents are responsible for picking up their own children. The elementary curriculum has been designed to meet state competencies as assessed by the State Wide Assessment Test (SWAT). Consequently, the coordinated curricula are progressive and each year's skills are based on knowledge acquired the previous year. Highlights of the school year include Grandparents'

Day, Recognition of the "Students of the Month," safety squad training, and the fundraiser to support a community service project. Past projects have included feeding a giraffe at the zoo for a year and planting a tree in the Brazilian rain forest. DCES has received academic honors. Outside of school, numerous students won ribbons at the county fair for 4-H projects, including prize sheep, biggest vegetable, and sewing.

Special Education Programs and Services
Students identified with disabilities have a full continuum of services available to them depending on their educational needs and the severity of the disability. Services listed below are either available in the district or through the BRESA.

Speech-Language Pathologists: Speech and language pathologists are available for students from 3 through 21 years of age. Services include direct therapy (various models are used), consultation with parents and staff, membership on Individualized Education Program Teams (IEPT), and diagnostic evaluation of individual student's speech and language.

School Psychologists: School psychologists are available for students from 3 through 21 years of age. Services include assessment of learning and emotional problems, membership on Individualized Education Program Teams (IEPT), classroom observations, and consultation with parents and staff, short-term direct therapy with students, and assistance with alternative programming for students.

Social Workers: School social workers are available for students from 3 through 21 years of age. Service include evaluation for possible emotional problems, consultation to parents and staff, membership on Individualized Education Program Teams (IEPT), direct service to students, and referral to outside agencies to meet a variety of student needs (including resources for clothing, food, housing, mental health, glasses, etc.)

School Nurses: School nurses are available for students from 3 through 21 years of age. Services include monitoring health records; arranging for vision, hearing, and dental screenings; and membership on Individual Education Program Teams (IEPT) when appropriate. They also serve as liaisons between the hospital and school for some children with serious health impairments. The nurses work with families on a variety of health programs including lice, pink eye, etc.

Occupational Therapists and Physical Therapists: Occupational and physical therapists are based at the Fernald Center (see below), but are available for assessment, consultation, membership on Individualized Education Program Teams

(IEPT), and some direct service as identified on Individual Educational Programs (IEPs). Direct services promote muscle control, muscle motion, and the development of self-help skills. Adaptive equipment recommendations may also be made.

Teacher Consultants: State-certified teacher consultants for students with learning disabilities, emotional impairments, and mental retardation are employed by the Dewey Consolidated Schools. These special education professionals are itinerant staff and provide consultant services for students or teachers as specified on IEPs. For students with visual impairments, physical impairments, and hearing impairments, the teacher consultants are hired by the BRESA and are generally available on a contract basis to meet needs identified on IEPs. Teacher consultant services are available at the elementary, middle, and high school level.

Augmentative and Assistive Technology Consultant: This consultant is hired by the BRESA and provides the district with expertise in assistive technology and augmentative and alternative communication devices. The consultant, based in the instructional media center, maintains a library of equipment that may be borrowed on a trial basis by local districts prior to purchase. The consultant has expertise in the use of low-cost modifications and more complex high-end technology. Services provided by the consultant include technology assessments, recommendations on usage, and trial use of equipment. The consultant is also available to serve on an IEPT when necessary.

Transition Specialist: A state-endorsed transition specialist is available through BRESA. This person offers expertise in assisting local districts in writing the students transition plan. The transition specialist also serves as a liaison to state vocational planning commission and other community resources. The transition specialist is also available to serve on an IEPT when necessary.

Resource Rooms: Cross-categorical resource rooms are available at the elementary, middle, and high school levels. These special education classrooms provide pullout services for students with various disabilities. The special education teachers are available to provide co-teaching options with general educators. Typically, this service is available for students for no more than one half their school day.

Self-Contained Classrooms: For students that require a more restrictive environment, DCSD has hired teachers for self-contained at the elementary and middle school level. For self-contained classrooms with more than fifteen students, a teaching assistant is also assigned. The district does have a cooperative arrangement with a neighboring school district. Dewey Consolidated Schools has a program for students who need a specialized functional curriculum and typically are learners with moderate to severe mental retardation. The neighboring district offers a program for students that need a consistent structure and a small class. Typically these children have severe communication delays, behavioral difficulties, and cognitive impairments. These programs are available for students aged 3 to 21 years of age.

Day School Programs: BRESA offers intensive center-based programs for students who have more severe disabilities. Typically students attending the Fernald Center are identified as eligible for special education support as students with severe mentally retardation, severe multiple impairments, and autistic spectrum disorders. Physical therapy, occupational therapy, nursing support, and speech therapy are available on site. BRESA also offers a day treatment program for students with serious emotional impairments who cannot be successfully programmed for by the local districts. The Morse School is available for students K–12, and through a cooperative arrangement with the Department of Mental Health, offers psychological and social work services on site. Speech and language therapy is also available.

Residential Schools: The state runs residential schools for students who are blind and deaf to assist in learning basic skills. Binet Lake Hospital also offers an educational program for children who have serious health or physical problems that require and extended hospitalizations.

Homebound Services: Homebound services are available for those students who, for a variety of reasons, cannot profit from a school experience or cannot physically be accommodated in school due to serious health problems.

Preschool Services: For students identified as having disabilities before school age, DCS offers a home-based program for children 0 to 2 years of age. From ages 3 to 6, a pre-primary impaired classroom in available. A full-time speech pathologist is assigned to work with this program. Support from social work, school psychology, and nursing staff is available as needed.

Vocational and Technical Center (Voc. Center): A regional vocational center is operated by BRESA for general and special education students who are preparing for a vocation or career upon high school graduation. Courses are available in basic job skills as well as more advanced training. Opportunities at the Voc. Center include auto repair and electrical systems, horticulture, food preparation and catering, cosmetology, cleaning and maintenance, welding, basic carpentry, and childcare. Other opportunities are available through job coaching, job shadowing, mentoring, and other arrangements with members of the community.

2 Individual with a Learning Disability

How can two students with similar needs not receive the same services?

Characters: Linda Robbins, fourth-grade teacher

Maggie Bracken, fourth-grade student

Mr. and Mrs. Bracken, Maggie's parents

Liz Shuler, fourth-grade student

Mrs. Shuler, Liz's mother

Gemma, Jamal, Hector, Jason, Heather, Susan, Glory (classmates)

Edna Ewell, principal

Rick McDonald, LD teacher, resource room

Marsha Matchwick, school psychologist

Flashpoint

Mrs. Robbins did not understand it, nor was she sure how she could explain it at upcoming parent conferences. Maggie and Liz had been best friends since kindergarten, attended the same school, struggled with reading and had come to rely on each other for moral support when reading was difficult for them. Both girls knew the names of the letters of the alphabet and a few sight words, but both could not read text more difficult than the early second-grade level. Now that they were in fourth grade, they needed grade-level reading skills or individualized teaching to learn the content for the other subjects.

Mrs. Robbins reflected on her class. The State Wide Achievement Test (SWAT) was also rapidly approaching and the girls were really going to struggle with those state-mandated tests. Gemma Wagomen, Jamal Warner, and Maggie and Liz were the students she worried most about not passing the SWAT. The results of those tests had implications for the school district funding formula. The results of the recent evaluations completed on both girls indicated that Liz was learning disabled and Maggie was not eligible for any special education services.

Mrs. Robbins wanted some answers and she wanted them now. It wasn't fair that Liz would be eligible for special education services and not Maggie. In the classroom, both girls were reading at the same level, and Maggie needed help as much as Liz. Mrs. Robbins knew that special education services might include direct instruction from the LD teacher, assistance for Liz on tests, multisensory hands-on instructional materials, modified grading, and/or other accommodations that would encourage Liz to be a successful learner. As a bonus, Mr. McDonald was well liked by his students and he was someone she could talk to about how to work effectively with the LD children when she ran into a problem. Well, she for one was looking forward to the MET (multidisciplinary evaluation team) meetings after school. It would be a great opportunity to get some answers to this question and let the MET team know what it was like to be Liz's and Maggie's teacher.

Reader Inquiry and Reflection

- Based on what you've read so far, what questions do you have about this situation?
- What additional information is needed?
- What information about the school, community, or family might be relevant to this case?

Background

Because Maggie and Liz had difficulties reading in her class, Mrs. Robbins had reviewed their school records and discovered that the girls had been in class together since kindergarten. Previous teachers had noted that the girls were best friends and usually chose to play together and work together. Neither was reading by the end of second grade and both had been considered for retention. However, that had not occurred. In third grade the teacher had assigned a parent volunteer to work with the girls, but that had not noticeably improved their skills. By the end of third grade the girls knew the letter names and some sight words, but were not fluent readers. On classroom reading assignments and teacher-made tests both girls were functioning at the same reading level, about second grade.

Liz lived in a single-parent household. Her parents divorced when she was a toddler and her father lived in another town with his second wife and their children. Her mother worked full time cleaning offices, but money was a constant problem in the family. Liz and her mother live in a low-income housing project. With the near poverty level income, Liz qualified for free breakfast and lunch at school. However, education was valued in the Shuler home and Mrs. Shuler made sure that

Liz did her homework and was in school on time. Mrs. Shuler indicated that it often took Liz a long time to complete even simple assignments and Mrs. Shuler had to work intensely with her.

The results of the recent evaluation indicated that on the Wechsler Intelligence Scale for Children-Third Edition (WISC-III), Liz earned a Verbal Score of 88, a Performance Score of 113, and a Full Scale Score of 101. These scores are based on an average of 100 and compare Liz to other students her age. The test results indicate that when solving problems that are related to school success, Liz scores in the average range, but her nonverbal skills are better than her verbal ones. When given an achievement test, her scores on the same scale were Reading 82, Math 99, Spelling 78, and General Information 100. The report indicated that Math and General Information were in the average range while Reading and Spelling were significantly below expected levels. The Full Scale Score on the WISC-III is used to set expected levels of achievement. The difference between Liz's Reading Score of 82 and the Full Scale Score of 101 met the school district guideline for severe discrepancy between ability and achievement. Specific strengths identified included motor skills, social skills, general information, listening skills, and math. Specific weaknesses included unable to use phonics skills to decode words, low reading comprehension, letter confusions (i.e., b and d, W and M), and difficulty with sound-symbol association.

Mr. McDonald, the special education teacher with expertise in learning disabilities, had already started to think about ways to assist Mrs. Robbins with teaching Liz. He mentioned that it might be a good time to try the team teaching they had been talking about. Also he knew of a computer program that would reinforce some of the science and social studies content that was being taught in the fourth grade, particularly the American history unit that Mrs. Robbins always taught.

Maggie lived with her parents and an older sister a few blocks away from the Shulers. Maggie's mother stopped teaching when she had children and stayed home with the girls. Mr. Bracken continues to teach at the high school in a neighboring district. The family looks forward to an annual summer vacation; they usually rent a cottage for two weeks in the northern part of the state. The Brackens are concerned about Maggie's lack of reading progress and readily gave permission for the evaluation. In addition, they have hired a tutor to work with Maggie once a week.

The results of the recent evaluation indicated that on the Wechsler Intelligence Scale for Children-Third Edition (WISC-III), Maggie earned a Verbal Score of 79, a Performance Score of 84, and a Full Scale Score of 82. These scores are based on an average of 100 just as Liz's scores are. This indicates that when solving problems that are related to school success, Maggie scores in the below average range, and her nonverbal skills are not statistically different than her verbal ones. When given an achievement test, her scores on the same test and using the same scale as Liz, were Reading 82, Math 85, Spelling 78, and General Information 82. The report indicated that in all areas tested, Maggie scored in the below average range. There was no discrepancy between expected levels of achievement and actual achievement. Specific strengths identified included motor skills and social skills (successful member of her afterschool soccer team, but she tends to follow the lead of other students). Specific weaknesses noted include the inability to use phonics skills to decode words, low reading comprehension, and difficulty with sound-symbol association. Maggie also wrote neatly, appeared organized, and could copy from the board.

Mrs. Robbins thought about what she would say to the families in their separate meetings that afternoon. She planned to report that in the classroom, both girls are having difficulty with reading, which is also impacting other subject areas such as science and social studies. Mrs. Robbins indicates that she tries to use as many different methods of teaching as possible, often using culminating experiences and teamwork instead of traditional tests. An example is the unit for American history. This project was difficult because they were unable to read. However, Mrs. Robbins noted that because of her good listening skills, Liz was able to contribute more to her group than Maggie contributed to her group. Socially, both girls are rather quiet and tend to keep to themselves. Some of the students teased them and called them "Dumb and Dumber" and "retard" at the beginning of the year. However, Mrs. Robbins reported she would not accept such behavior from her class and to her knowledge the teasing has stopped. After all, neither girl is "stupid." Mrs. Robbins went on to say that both girls needed intensive one-to-one help by a trained teacher to learn the keys to reading—even the small group instruction in the regular class had not been successful. Furthermore, in third grade, the teacher had assigned a parent volunteer to work with the girls and that had not improved their reading skills significantly either. Mrs. Robbins would also mention that she was truly worried about the future school success of these students without some intervention.

Continuation and Closure

The two MET meetings were held that afternoon. Mrs. Robbins, Mr. McDonald, Mrs. Matchwick, and Mrs. Ewell were at both. Mr. and Mrs. Bracken attended the first meeting about Maggie, and Mrs. Shuler came after work to be at the second. Since Maggie and Liz were best friends, the families knew each other quite well. Both sets of parents were aware that both girls had been tested. The meetings were to review the test results, listen to concerns of the parents, consider input from Mrs. Robbins, and decide if there was enough information to determine if either child was eligible for special education services and to schedule an IEP meeting. If the child were not eligible, then the MET would try to develop a plan for that student.

Questions/Activity/Task

- How could Mrs. Robbins or the other professionals explain to Maggie's parents why one girl was receiving special education services and the other was not?
- Consider the legal and ethical implications of confidentiality. Does this change your response to question 1?
- What educational programming suggestions would your team recommend for Maggie? Why?
- Could Mrs. Robbins simply use whatever modifications were suggested for Liz with Maggie? Would technology help in this situation?

3 Individual with Attention Deficit Hyperactivity Disorder

Alphonso's disruptive behavior was a challenge to his parents, teachers, and peers.

Characters: Alphonso Young, 4-year-old Head Start student

Mr. and Mrs. Young, Alphonso's parents

Susan Cross, Head Start teacher

Lynn Cybulski, Fernald Center pre-primary specialist

Shirley Spires, teacher of school-based preschool and latchkey program

Marsha Matchwick, school psychologist, DCSD

Rory Johnson, 4-year-old Head Start student

Flashpoint

Ms. Cross saw the big tower out of the corner of her eye. "Oh, oh," she thought, "where's Alphonso?" Alphonso had just noticed that Rory had built a big tower from the cardboard blocks in the block area. Before Ms. Cross could get across the room, Alphonso had jumped up, knocked down the blocks, and taken as many as he could hold. Rory started crying, tried to get the blocks back, and in the process hit Alphonso on the arm. Alphonso in turn quickly hit back and his hand caught Rory on the cheek. By this time, Ms. Cross was kneeling down between her students and trying to settle things down. As she looked up, she realized the school psychologist had just walked into the room and observed the whole interaction. Ms. Cross breathed a sigh of relief and thought, "At least Ms. Matchwick will understand what I've been talking about."

Reader Inquiry and Reflection

- What might Ms. Cross be talking about?
- Based on what you've read so far, what questions do you have about this situation?
- What additional information is needed?
- What information about the school, community, or family might be relevant to this case?

Background

Head Start is a federally sponsored compensatory program for low-income children prior to kindergarten enrollment. Head Start provides comprehensive services to eligible children and their families. These services include health, education, social services and parental involvement. About 10 percent of the spaces available are for children eligible for special education. The teachers and teacher assistants may have completed some community college work or have an associate degree, but are not necessarily certified teachers as defined by state requirements. Head Start children are bussed one way to school; parents have to provide transportation the other way.

Ms. Cross was concerned about a child in her Head Start class. Alphonso seemed to want to be with other children and play with them. But when he approached children, it was usually to grab toys or to push the kids. When she talked to Alphonso, he seemed genuinely sorry that he did not follow the rules, but two minutes later he would do the same thing. Alphonso seemed to have all the age-appropriate learning skills, in fact, his fine and gross motor skills were better than most of the children in her program. The bus driver also said that Alphonso got into trouble on the bus and he now had to sit up front right behind the driver. Ms. Cross had also noted and documented that Alphonso did not stick with any activity for more than a minute or two. He seemed to spend most of his time wandering around the classroom and taking a toy out for a minute then putting it down anywhere he happened to be. He also had difficulty sitting for circle time, unless he was next to the teacher, the aide, or one of the volunteer moms. When he was with an adult, he would usually participate in activities for a few minutes. The other children in the class have started to avoid him and don't want him to play with them. When asked about it, Rory said, "He doesn't play right."

Ms. Cross, with Mrs. Young's permission, had asked the school psychologist to observe Alphonso in the classroom and see if she had any ideas. Ms. Matchwick had indicated that she would also like to speak with Mrs. Young. That interview was scheduled immediately after the observation. Mrs. Young had agreed to come about a half hour before she had to pick up Alphonso, but she was bringing the baby, because she did not want to hire a sitter and her husband was sleeping.

Alphonso was a 4-year-old boy. He was the middle of three children in the Young family. Alphonso's older sister Tamika was in kindergarten and his younger brother Jerome was 3 months old. Mr. Young worked part-time evenings for an office cleaning company. His hours varied from 10 to 45 hours per week, depending on the needs of his boss. He worked enough hours to cover expenses, but because he was not full-time, he was ineligible for employer-paid medical benefits for him or his family. Mr. Young hoped to be made full-time as soon as the company found additional clients. The family received food stamps to supplement their income and Tamika was eligible for free breakfast at school, while Alphonso received breakfast at Head Start. Mrs. Young stayed home and raised the children.

During the interview, Mrs. Young affectionately called Alphonso her "wild child." Even as a baby Alphonso was more active than either of her other children. At first she thought he was just "all boy." She indicated that she has very little control over Alphonso, although he does listen better to her husband. However, because it is important that her husband be able to sleep during the day, she does almost anything to keep Alphonso quiet and away from her sleeping husband. She indicated that Alphonso likes to watch cartoons and videos and she frequently lets him spend the afternoon watching his shows. She further stated that with other toys he quickly loses interest and just throws them around the room. Mrs. Young also observed that Alphonso does not usually play well with his sister and often gets mad at the baby when he cries. In fact, she added that her sisters (Alphonso's aunts) will no longer let him come over to play with his cousins and her parents will not let Alphonso visit their house without his dad. She explained that Alphonso gets so excited that he just runs through their homes, jumps on furniture, and disrupts everything.

On the other hand, Mrs. Young said that when Alphonso is settled down, he is the most loving boy she had ever seen. He also really liked stuffed animals, he would rub the fur and snuggle with his stuffed bear when he watched television and for the six or seven hours he would sleep at night.

When Alphonso went to the free clinic for his physical and immunizations for Head Start, the nurse had suggested that Mrs. Young might want Alphonso to see his own pediatrician or a specialist because he was so wound up in the waiting room he disturbed everyone who was there. Mrs. Young indicated she simply said yes and took the name. She did not follow up and was embarrassed to say they could not afford another visit to the doctor. Mrs. Young indicated that after the nurse's comments and watching an "Oprah" show on children with attention problems, she though Alphonso might be ADHD. ADHD describes students who display hyperactive behaviors, have difficulty attending to the task at hand, and tend to be impulsive. These characteristics may be demonstrated in various ways in different situations.

Continuation and Closure

After the observation and interview, Ms. Matchwick agreed with Mrs. Young and Ms. Cross that Alphonso is a challenging child who may be ADHD. They decide that something needs to be done soon to assist Alphonso in learning how to interact with children and adapt successfully to the classroom experience.

Questions/Activity/Task

- What should the next steps be for Ms. Cross, Mrs. Young and Ms. Matchwick? Are there other community or school resources that should be involved?
- If Alphonso is ADHD, would he be eligible for additional educational support? Why?
- To what extent should the interventions designed for Alphonso include his behavior at home? How can communication between family and school be facilitated?
- What kinds of support would be appropriate for Alphonso? (Hint: Think about help for Ms. Cross, classroom modifications, special education, or some other arrangement.)
- List one or two things that Ms. Cross could do immediately while the steps you have outlined above are implemented.

CHAPTER

4 Individual with Speech and Language Impairments

How can teachers evaluate Michelle's readiness for kindergarten if no one but her mother can understand a single thing she says?

Characters: Michelle Alvarez, 4 years old

Roberto and Maria Alvarez, parents

Kate Ling, Fernald Center pre-primary impaired teacher

Tyrell Owen, speech-language pathologist

Celia Haddad, DCSD kindergarten teacher

Lynn Cybulski, Fernald Center pre-primary specialist

Flashpoint

"Remember," Kate Ling chided herself, "she's speaking as clearly as she can and she is trying to communicate." Kate sighed deeply, masking her impatience with a smile and said, "OK, Michelle, please tell me one more time." Little Michelle Alvarez, at least equally frustrated, tried again to make her wishes known. "Aah ohn a aab hey ow," said Michelle. (I want the baby doll.) Kate remained clueless, and finally Michelle moved Kate out of the way, climbed up on a chair, and retrieved the doll from a shelf where it had been inadvertently placed earlier in the day. This was only the most recent example of a litany of exchanges that had taken place during the ten days since the beginning of the winter semester.

"That sweet little girl must hate coming to school, and quite honestly, Lynn, I know I start to cringe inside when I see her start to open her mouth." Kate was sharing her morning frustrations over a cup of tea and a muffin in the teachers' lounge. Her colleague, Lynn Cybulski, also a pre-primary impaired specialist shook her head sympathetically. "When is the speech pathologist coming to consult with you?" Lynn asked. "Soon, I hope, for your sake as well as Michelle's. "Thankfully," answered Kate, "Tyrell Owen and I are meeting tomorrow afternoon. He's the new speech/language pathologist they hired away from Binet Lake Hospital. He has an excellent reputation."

Back in her classroom, preparing for the afternoon session, Kate continued to ponder Michelle Alvarez and her severe speech disorder. From what she had heard, Tyrell Owen had tons of experience with a variety of clients in many different settings. "Good," thought Kate, "Michelle and I need all the help we can get." Kate remembered that she was the person responsible for assessing Michelle's readiness for kindergarten and she thought about how difficult that would be when Michelle's speech was not understandable. "I will need to think creatively for this evaluation to be successful." Kate said to herself.

Reader Inquiry and Reflection

- Based on what you've read so far, what questions do you have about this situation?
- What additional information is needed?
- What information about the school, community, or family might be relevant to this case?

Background

The Alvarez family lives in a middle-class subdivision in Binet Lake. Roberto Alvarez is a salesperson for a plastics company; he travels a lot in his work and is generally away from home fifteen to twenty days each month. Maria Alvarez is a highly successful realtor; however, she has severely curtailed her business activities since Michelle's surgery and severe speech problems. Maria and Roberto were both born in Binet Lake. Despite their Spanish heritage, both parents speak only English.

Until she had hernia surgery the previous summer, Michelle Alvarez was the prototype of a typical 4-year-old. Due to an unexpected problem during the surgery, Michelle suffered cardiac arrest and the resulting oxygen deprivation created a cerebral insult. In other words, at the age of 4, Michelle Alvarez had a stroke. Following her recovery from surgery, Michelle's condition was thoroughly evaluated by a team of specialists at Binet Lake Hospital. Michelle is ambulatory with normal hearing and vision. Her gross motor skills are excellent, but her fine motor coordination is slightly below average. Michelle is cognitively within the average range. The primary disability resulting from the stroke is a severe motor speech disorder. Michelle's articulation is severely slurred. She produces appropriate intonation and her sentences appear to be linguistically correct, but Michelle is virtually unintelligible. In addition to the motor speech disorder, Michelle has a mild language delay that is most often demonstrated in her comprehension of oral directions. It is not known whether the language delay existed prior to her stroke.

As a result of an IEPT meeting held in the fall, Michelle began receiving speech therapy and preschool programming at the Fernald Center.

Before the stroke Michelle loved to talk and sing. She still does. Roberto and Maria Alvarez are very concerned that Michelle's speech disorder will interfere with her academic achievement and social development. In a recent conversation with a DCSD social worker, Maria commented, "I understand her, but those teachers . . . how can they know how smart Michelle is if they can't understand anything she says?"

Michelle's social development has also been adversely effected. Prior to the surgery, Michelle had lots friends her own age from around her neighborhood and from her church community. Since the stroke, Michelle's social world has narrowed drastically. She plays by herself, with her parents, or occasionally with a cousin. Sadly, her peers can't understand her any better than her teachers. Moreover, based on her unintelligible speech, many parents in the neighborhood have decided that Michelle is retarded. Out of ignorance and fear, they isolate Michelle and shower Maria and Roberto with their pity.

Continuation and Closure

During the first thirty minutes of the meeting, Tyrell Owen discussed his findings from a detailed evaluation of Michelle and also reviewed information from her hospital file. During the meeting, Kate and Celia asked a few questions but mostly listened to Mrs. Alvarez and Mr. Owen and took their own notes. Kate invited Celia Haddad to the meeting because if Michelle were assigned to a regular education kindergarten class next year, Celia would be her teacher. Mr. and Mrs. Alvarez had also been invited because parents can provide valuable insights about communication strategies at home. Celia and Kate had worked together for years and Kate knew that Celia was a teacher committed to the success of all children. Celia appreciated the invitation and responded by saying, "If Michelle is going to be in my classroom, I want to begin planning for her right now." Kate also intended to include Celia in the process and decision concerning a recommendation about Michelle's kindergarten readiness. Kate and Celia knew from experience that early and consistent collaboration benefited their students. Michelle wasn't the first student and she wouldn't be the last student that they worked with collaboratively.

Kate liked Tyrell. He was honest and he had some specific recommendations. "Some aspects of Michelle's speech disorder—the drooling, for instance—I think we can improve over the next several months with oral motor exercises and verbal cues. Unfortunately, her speech will likely continue to be difficult to understand for a considerable time period, but we can provide her with an alternative." Tyrell gave an overview of the two augmentative communication systems he thought should be utilized. The first was a portable voice output system that Michelle could take everywhere. Regardless of manufacturer, these systems provide multiple overlays for a touch panel that can assemble, remember, and activate voice messages. In addition, the voices for these systems are created for individual clients. For Michelle," said Tyrell, "the voice would be that of a preschool female."

The second system Tyrell recommended was a series of nonelectronic communication charts that could be laminated and placed at a number of appropriate stations at home and in school. For example, in school, there would be a chart for art, science, numbers, music, etc. Each chart contains a series of pictographic symbols and words. Tyrell provided them a paper copy of a sample (attached). "Even though the parents insist they understand Michelle's utterances, I hope they will consider these systems for home as well. I found this article written for parents about augmentative and assistive communication in the home. "I hope all of you have a chance to read it before we meet again next week to make a decision."

Although the electronic voice output system would need to be designed and ordered, the communication charts could be implemented almost immediately. In addition, Tyrell consulted with Kate about a schedule for three pullout sessions a week where he could work with Michelle on oral-motor exercises. The three educators and the parents agreed that the language delay was so mild that they would wait and address it after some of the other communication strategies had been implemented. That was fine with Kate. She was elated over the possibility of truly being able to interact with Michelle. "Plus," thought Kate, "any card-carrying, crumb-grinding 4-year-old will think the pictograph charts and voice output technology are 'way cool'—for once, Michelle will be the star!"

Kate was still worried about conducting a fair assessment of kindergarten readiness, but she knew she could count on Tyrell and Celia. For the first time since Michelle joined her classroom, Kate felt as though she could begin to respond to Michelle's needs and help her grow and develop.

Questions/Activity/Task

- Should Maria and Roberto Alvarez be encouraged to use augmentative communication at home even though they understand Michelle's speech? Why or why not?
- Should Michelle be encouraged to use her own voice in addition to augmentative communication? Why or why not? Suggest strategies that Kate Ling can implement to promote the desired behavior.
- Based on Michelle's disability, what accommodations in the kindergarten readiness assessment process should Kate Ling and Celia Haddad consider? Should the criteria be the same? Why or why not?
- When should the mild language delay be addressed in the IEP? Why do you think the educators and parents chose not to focus on this issue now?

hello	good morning	goodbye	good night
guess what!	Ha Ha Ha	Have a nice day	Have you heard
I agree	I don't want	desk items	paste
easel	envelope	fasteners	paints
glitter	markers	masking tape	stamp

Mayer-Johnson Co., P.O. Box 1579, Solana Beach, CA 92075

CHAPTER

5 Individual with Mental Retardation

Shirley and Charles Judd want what's best for their grandson, but they are not convinced that the teachers are correct about J.J.'s achieving self-sufficiency as an adult.

Characters: Jeremy Judd (J.J.), 16-year-old tenth grade student

Shirley and Charles Judd, grandparents

Lucy Turcott, BRESA Transition Specialist

Elliot Santi, high school resource room teacher

Flashpoint

All in all, it had been a pleasant home visit, just not as productive as he had hoped. Shirley and Charles Judd seemed somewhat surprised when Elliot Santi suggested the informal meeting prior to the annual review. They were immediately concerned that something else had gone wrong with J.J. and school. Elliot reassured them, "J.J.'s doing just fine; in fact, we think he is ready for a community placement along with his course work. That's what we need to discuss." The Judds (both retired) lived in a small, aging home located in one of the poorer neighborhoods in Kirk. Both the home and the yard had received a lot of loving care over the years and Elliot's welcome included a fresh pot of coffee along with a delicious homemade rhubarb pie. J.J.'s grandparents had been his legal guardians since he was 4; they loved him dearly and were always supportive of him "taking care of business at school." However, they were also very protective. Elliot believed that their sorrow and grief over J.J.'s "condition," as they referred to his disability, caused them to focus more on J.J.'s limitations than his possibilities. As Shirley said after Elliot explained the community-based horticultural program, "That boy is as sweet as he is slow and he doesn't need any more heartache and disappointment."

Elliot knew that the Judds were the most important influence in J.J.'s life; he would do anything to fulfill his grandparents' expectations. Actually, it was Charles' careful and patient teaching in the backyard garden that had nurtured J.J.'s interest in plants and flowers. The staff at the Voc. Center believed that with the right training and experience J.J.'s transition into adulthood could include a career in horticulture that would accord him a measure of self-sufficiency. "I should have mentioned the possible job opportunities on those huge farms out in Lehtinen Township," Elliot thought as he drove back to the Voc. Center. "I wonder if we have any graduates working out there whose profiles are similar to J.J.'s? I'll check with Lucy Turcott when we meet this afternoon. J.J. can make it—I know he can. Somehow the grandparents have to believe that challenging J.J. may be more important than protecting him. After all, both Shirley and Charles are in their seventies and . . . "

Reader Inquiry and Reflection

- Based on what you've read so far, what questions do you have about this situation?
- What additional information is needed?
- What information about the school, community, or family might be relevant to this case?

Background

Jeremy Judd (J.J.) was an only child, born prematurely, weighing only slightly over three pounds at birth and suffering from fetal alcohol syndrome. His mother, Dolores, received very poor prenatal care; she had been laid off from her job at a paper factory and her health benefits expired early in her pregnancy. At that time, Dolores was estranged from her parents and Shirley and Charles Judd were not aware of their daughter's economic and medical circumstances. Dolores worked hard at a variety of part-time jobs to support her son. Neighbors and friends cared for J.J. while his mother was working. Because he was an only child and none of his volunteer caregivers had children his age, J.J.'s delayed language and fine/gross motor skill development remained unnoticed. He also displayed less curiosity and exploration than his age cohorts. J.J. preferred playing by himself. When with other children, J.J. participated in parallel rather than social play. Dolores was killed in an automobile accident when J.J. was 4 years old. In addition to mourning the loss of their only child, Shirley and Charles Judd became parents to a grandson they had never met.

During the first eighteen months with his grandparents, J.J.'s developmental deficiencies were credited to the trauma of losing his mother as well as having to adjust to a new living situation. Under such circumstances, no one was terribly alarmed when J.J. was retained in kindergarten for a second year. When J.J.'s language, motor, social, and cognitive development showed only marginal improvement during his second year in kindergarten, his teacher consulted with the Judds and initiated a referral to special education. As a result of the special education evaluation, J.J. was diagnosed as mentally retarded with an IQ of 64 and adaptive skill deficiencies in functional academics, social skills, and communication. His hearing was fine but he was fitted with corrective lenses following a vision exam. During the elementary grades, J.J.'s individualized educational programs provided for two sessions each week with a speech-language pathologist. Generally speaking, J.J.'s school time was divided equally between the resource room and the general education classroom. J.J.'s teachers primarily designed his instruction using hands-on activities and created opportunities for practicing social skills by placing J.J. in cooperative groups with positive, interactive classmates. Shirley and Charles Judd rejoiced with each of J.J.'s accomplishments and silently wept through each insult and disappointment. J.J.'s speech and language skills were commensurate with cognition and individual speech and language therapy was discontinued in the sixth grade. Since the eighth grade, his IEPs have included a transition plan. A vocational assessment conducted during ninth grade concluded that J.J. had the potential to become self-sufficient and recommended a transition to adulthood program combining basic academic skills with career development in the horticultural sciences.

Now in the tenth grade, J.J.'s social skills have improved significantly since early elementary but he doesn't date and has much less social interaction than his peers. Academically, his reading comprehension is at the fourth-grade level, oral reading and vocabulary skills are at the seventh grade level. J.J.'s math scores are higher than those in reading; he has good numerical skills. All of J.J.'s high school teachers report that he follows directions well, has good personal hygiene, is punctual, and has a pleasant, cooperative attitude. His IEP provides for a half day at the high school for academic subjects and the attendance at an exploratory program at the Voc. Center for the remainder of the school day.

J.J. spends two hours a day at the Voc. Center learning general workplace skills in the areas of task responsibility, following directions, customer service, safety, and communication. At the Voc. Center he has the opportunity to learn a little about different vocational skills including horticulture, machine repair, welding, cleaning and maintenance, and food services. At the beginning of the year Mr. Santi had talked with J.J. about what he wanted to do after high school. J.J. indicated that he wanted to work and live alone. J.J. talked about his interests in baseball, plants, and bugs. J.J. indicated he liked to work outside when the weather was good.

Throughout J.J.'s schooling, Shirley and Charles Judd have never missed an IEPT or a parent-teacher conference. Both the Judds are grateful for the resources available to J.J. through the DCSD and BRESA. From time to time, however, they have been reluctant to support changes in J.J.'s IEP, which they felt might make him vulnerable to public review, criticism, and failure. Each of these prior issues had been successfully resolved and J.J. had ultimately triumphed over each new challenge.

J.J.'s grandparents are very resistant to the idea of a community job placement and have withheld approval for that portion of next year's IEP. They are fearful, not wanting to create expectations within J.J. that they believe could never be realized.

Continuation and Closure

"Well?" quizzed Lucy Turcott before the coffee cups were full and before either she or Elliot were seated. "Well," responded Elliot, "we have a lot of work to do if we are going to get the Judds to approve community-based placement for J.J." "I think the bottom line is that they don't really believe that J.J. can become self-supporting, either living on his own or even in a group setting." Over the next hour Elliot and Lucy thoroughly reviewed J.J.'s file and Elliot shared in detail his impressions from his morning visit with Shirley and Charles Judd. Lucy slowly shook her head in wonder and disbelief as Elliot restated the Judds commitment to finding a restricted group home where J.J. could live after they both died or were incapacitated. "Of course," said Elliot, "they don't realize that those kinds of placements simply don't exist in this state any more, even if that was what J.J. needed." Before leaving to meet his one o'clock class, Elliot and Lucy agreed to spend the next few days putting together two plans. First, to try and demonstrate to the Judds that the work placement for J.J. would do more good than harm, and second, to carefully design the criteria for J.J.'s vocational placement so that he would succeed and his grandparents' leap of faith would be rewarded.

Questions/Activity/Task

- What strategies would you recommend that Elliot and Lucy utilize in trying to secure the Judds' approval for a community job placement for J.J.?
- Assume that you are members of the team creating the criteria for J.J.'s community job placement. Based on his background, strengths, weaknesses, level of preparation, etc., consider the following issues: type of placement (farm, landscaping, retail sales); working alone with trees, plants, and flowers or as part of a team; level and type of supervision required; recommended level of responsibility; recommended type of routine and structure; level and type of academic work to accompany the placement.

- What kinds of classes should J.J. be scheduled to take during his half-day at the high school? How should those classes be taught?
- Discuss the types of living situations that would be appropriate for J.J. upon completion of his high school program or when he turned 21 years of age.
- Based on the requirements specified in IDEA, what would the transition plan for J.J. look like for his eleventh-grade year?
- Should the transition plan address issues of socialization and recreation activities? If so, what would you suggest?

6 Individual with Academic Talent and Gifts

A student who was described by a former teacher as "sweet, but a reluctant learner" surprises her teacher by earning a perfect score on the statewide assessment science test.

Characters:	Gemma Wagomen, fourth grader
	Linda Robbins, teacher
	Edna Ewell, principal
	Hector Jason, Susan, and Dori, classmates
	Stan and Anna Wagomen, parents
	Rose Benet, maternal grandmother

Flashpoint

Linda Robbins grabbed the stack of paper from the corner of her desk before heading to the teachers' lounge. She might as well sort through the pile of reports, notices, and memos while she munched her tuna salad sandwich. Thankfully, her thirty-one fourth graders were in the capable hands of the lunchroom and playground aides. She needed a break; it had been a frustrating morning. No specific problem or disaster, it just seemed that nothing had gone according to plan (group work!). As she entered the lounge, Linda greeted her colleagues, passed on the available table seating, and settled in one of the lounge chairs in the back of the room. "Strong, hot coffee, a little tuna salad, some mindless chatter, and I'll be ready to roll," she mused. Linda leafed through the material searching for a large, official-looking envelope. Edna Ewell told her that the SWAT (Statewide Achievement Test) results would be arriving today when she saw the principal greeting the busses earlier that morning. She was anxious to review the test results for her students. According to Edna, nine fourth graders achieved perfect scores on the science section of the exam—three in her class. "Twenty bucks says I know who the three are," Robbins thought as she scanned through the cumulative scores. "There's one, there's two, and number three should be . . . wait a minute . . . no, not Gemma. How could that be?" She was more than surprised. She was stunned.

Based on Linda's observations, Gemma Wagomen was a generally well-mannered, capable, but marginally motivated student. She certainly was not a high achiever in any subject, including science. Most of her grades were low Bs and Cs. In fact, Gemma was one of the sources of Linda's frustrating morning.

For the past week, during science and social studies, the students had been working on a project in cooperative groups. The project involved analyzing variables and proposing solutions to a hypothetical problem involving toxins discovered near a playground. The students were required to decide what poisons, debris, or other foreign objects might be found on the playground, decide a way to count how many harmful items, and think about ways to improve the environment. The activity is the culmination of a science and social studies unit that looked at impact of humans on the environment. Linda Robbins was quite proud when she created this interdisciplinary unit, but the implementation had been a bit rocky. Although her students had some experience in cooperative learning activities, this was the most ambitious unit of instruction she had attempted. While circulating and monitoring the groups this morning, Linda noted Gemma's disruption of her group's process and product. This was not the first time. Yesterday, Gemma seemed to totally withdraw from the group process and made no contribution to completing that day's task. Today she was active but certainly not helpful. Hector, Jason, Susan, and Dori complained that Gemma kept suggesting "silly" solutions or "other weird stuff." Linda asked Gemma to remain in class a few minutes while the other students went to gym and gently reprimanded her for not being a productive group member. Gemma, eyes staring at the floor, listened politely to her teacher's expectations and simply said "Yes, Ma'am."

Linda Robbins sat back in the chair, closed her eyes, and began sorting through all of the information she had on Gemma Wagomen. "A perfect SWAT score in science? Now that is a puzzle."

Reader Inquiry and Reflection

- Based on what you've read so far, what questions do you have about this situation?
- What additional information is needed?
- What information about the school, community, or family might be relevant to this case?

Background

The Wagomen family moved into the DCSD from a nearby two years ago, shortly after the death of Harry Benet, Gemma's maternal grandfather. The family (including an uncle and grandmother) lives in a rented trailer on the Kirk/Lehtinen Township border. Stan and Anna Wagomen are attentive and hard-working parents who value both informal and formal education. Gemma is the oldest of their three children. Since moving into the DCSD, both Stan and Anna have regularly participated in parent-teacher conferences and have attended PTO activities as their work schedule allows. Gemma's grades have been a concern to Anna and Stan; they cannot understand how a child who is so bright and creative at home can only earn Bs and Cs in school. Gemma's teachers report that she is an average student who does not always seem motivated.

Due to economic hardship neither parent graduated from high school, but they are self-taught and accomplished in many areas. Stan is a voracious reader and a regular patron of the public library, often bringing his children to the Sunday afternoon library activities. Anna has developed quite a reputation around the trailer park for being able to fix almost anything or at least be able to diagnose exactly what's wrong. Her skills in this area provide ongoing opportunities for temporary work, which is important since Stan and Anna's primary employment is as seasonal agricultural workers. Gemma's uncle also works on the Lehtinen farms. Both parents continually seek out additional work in order to help the family become economically self-sufficient. Currently, the Wagomens qualify for and need to accept food stamps, which is an embarrassment for the family. Rose Benet, Gemma's maternal grandmother, is the primary caretaker of the children and home. Rose is fluent in French and the Chippewa dialect, with English as a less-proficient third language. Consequently, the Wagomen children can understand and speak basic French and Chippewa in addition to English. Rose Benet is also the family's cultural curator, passing on the rich traditions, values, and history of the Native American cultures. Gemma is especially close to Rose, and nothing is more of a treat to the Wagomen children than a story from grandmother.

Continuation and Closure

After welcoming her students in from recess, Linda Robbins announced that the SWAT results confirmed what she already knew. "Congratulations to each and every one of you. You worked hard and did your very best—always something to be proud of!" Linda did not single out any students and their scores for special acknowledgement. She did not believe in fostering a competitive classroom atmosphere. The students knew that the SWAT results would be discussed during the upcoming parent-teacher conferences. As the students prepared for language arts, Linda thought, "I'd give a nickel to watch Gemma's face if I did announce the perfect scores. Would she be as surprised as I was?"

Linda spent the next few days carefully observing Gemma in and out of class. Indeed, her level of involvement resembled a roller coaster, ranging from distracted daydreaming to intense participation. Very often on the playground she would be captivating several younger children with some kind of conversation or demonstration. While her class was in gym with Mrs. Arcadia, Linda Robbins reviewed Gemma's school records. Although she had seen the file prior to the beginning of the school year, this time she was looking for more information about Gemma's progress in school and scores on other sections of the SWAT. She discovered that Gemma had not been retained but had missed 32 days of school last year and she had already been out 15 days this year. Her absences tended to cluster in the spring and fall. There was no explanation for the inconsistent attendance record, but it was interesting that Gemma was succeeding in school despite the absences. Gemma entered DCES late in second grade there were no previous SWAT results, however, current results placed her in the 97th percentile in math and slightly above grade level in basic reading skills and reading comprehension in addition to the perfect score in science. Records from the reservation school described Gemma as "unfocused" and "reluctant." "Well," Linda wondered, "is she reluctant or is she bored? And since we don't have any district program or services for TAG students, does it matter?"

Questions/Activity/Task

- How should Linda approach this topic at the parent-teacher conference?
- Would you categorize Gemma as TAG? Why or why not? Should Gemma be given an IQ test? Why or why not?
- Brainstorm a list of instructional options for responding to Gemma's needs as a student. Select the ones that could be implemented by Mrs. Robbins.
- Using the science/social studies project outlined in the case study, design modifications that Linda Robbins can implement for Gemma.
- If Gemma was attending a school in a district that provided a program for students with talents and gifts would your recommendation be different?

7 Individual with an Emotional Impairment or Behaviorial Disorder

Sarah can do the math work, but why won't she?

Characters: Sarah Goodard, eighth grader

Shawn Quinn, special education teacher

Lorie Sipple, mathematics teacher

Donna Bray, assistant principal

Margaret Hudson, school social worker

Flashpoint

Sarah was working on problems in her math class when without warning she shoved the book and her papers to the floor, shouted, "This is boring, and I'm not doing this any more!" This was the third time in ten days this had happened and Ms. Sipple told Sarah, as she agreed to in her behavioral contract, she needed to take the pass and go to Mr. Quinn's room immediately. She initially refused to go, shouting more defiant statements at her teacher. After about 5 minutes of what seemed like an eternity to Ms. Sipple, Sarah finally picked up the pass and stomped out of class. Ms. Sipple wondered if the math assignment was really boring, too hard, or if something else was bothering Sarah.

Reader Inquiry and Relection

- Based on what you've read so far, what questions do you have about this situation?
- What additional information is needed?
- What information about the school, community, or family might be relevant to this case?

Background

Sarah was currently eligible for special education services as a student with emotional impairments/behavior disorders. She had been receiving special education services since fifth grade. For two years she had been in a self-contained classroom, but her behavior and attitudes were improving, so the IEPT determined that she should receive some of her coursework in a general education classroom and work with the resource room teacher for half of the day. Currently, she receives math, gym, social studies, and science within general education classrooms. English and study skills were taught in the special education programs. She was a classmate of Blake Kwon's and both students were in Mr. Quinn's resource room.

The school social worker, Ms. Hudson, had been assigned to Sarah's elementary school as well the middle school. She was able to provide some background information about Sarah. From kindergarten through third grade, Sarah progressed at a typical rate. She learned to read and do grade level math. She had some friends in her class, but seemed shy and generally kept to herself. In the fourth grade things began to change. Initially, she would cry for no reason, and, when someone approached her, she would become angry and tell him or her to go away. She quit taking homework home and often did not turn in her papers that were completed in school. Her fourth-grade teacher was concerned and shared her concerns with Mrs. Goodard at a parent conference. Mrs. Goodard denied that there were problems at home. She indicated that as a single mom she had to work long hours to support the two of them, and Sarah was just seeking some attention. She assured the teacher that things would be better soon, because she had been dating a man since September and believed that they would be married soon. He had a good job and things would be easier at home.

However, a few weeks after the conference, Sarah came to school with serious cuts and bruises that were not explained. Mrs. Hudson and the elementary principal made a referral to protective services indicating they suspected that Sarah had been abused. After a lengthy investigation, protective services did remove Sarah from the home, stating that the new boyfriend had been abusing Sarah and the environment was not currently safe. Sarah was placed in foster care in another school district for the remainder of fourth grade. In foster care her behavior in the classroom and with the foster family steadily declined. She became angrier, defiant of authority, physically and verbally lashing out at adults and classmates. Finally, special education evaluation was completed and the IEPT determined that she was eligible for special education.

She was placed in a self-contained program with social work support services. She also received counseling through the foster care agency. Her behavior began to slowly improve. For fifth and sixth grade she remained with the foster family with supervised visits with her mother, and the counseling and social work services continued. At the beginning of seventh grade, she was returned to her mother. Her mother had completed the court-required parenting classes and the boyfriend was out of the picture. The transition had been rocky initially, but things seemed to be working out. Sarah's school behavior had improved and she began attending general education for one class. The counseling was discontinued when she returned to live with her mother, but the social work support once a week was continued. Then this year she was placed in the resource room and more general education classes.

The academic testing conducted at the end of seventh grade indicated that Sarah continued to have some delays in reading and language arts, but her math skills were slightly above grade level. As was noted previously, her aptitude on intelligence tests were in the average range. The primary concern continued to be how to assist Sarah to manage her behavior in the general education classroom. Her outbursts tended to frustrate teachers and alienate her peers.

Currently Sarah was on a behavior contract that encouraged her to act appropriately in class. The contract included sections on classroom behavior and completing assignments. She could earn points toward a reward of her choosing (special lunch at her favorite fast food restaurant, purchase of a CD, etc.). It also provided a method for her to leave the classroom if she was unable to follow the classroom rules, which is what Ms. Sipple had invoked. It appeared that the contract was no longer working and perhaps it was time to look for additional alternatives.

Continuation and Closure

After school that day, Ms. Sipple sought out Mr. Quinn. They decided that it was time for a team meeting to see what other ideas might work for Sarah. This was a critical time, because by next year a transition plan for high school would need to be started. Mr. Quinn and Ms. Sipple decided to invite the assistant principal, the social worker, and Mrs. Goodard to brainstorm ideas and if necessary modify the current contract. Some of the ideas that might be considered included modifying the math curriculum, modifying the grading system, changing the contract, incorporating more positive behavior supports, or altering her course schedule.

Questions/Activity/Tasks

Assume that you are participating in the team meeting and address the following issues:

- How seriously should Sarah's charge that the math work is boring be taken? Should the math work be accelerated for Sarah? What factors need to be taken into consideration before such a decision is made?

- Considering Sarah's age, are their other factors that may be influencing her behavior? How can the team investigate these potential influences?
- Should Sarah's behavioral contract be revised? Why or why not? What revisions would you recommend?
- Do you think that Sarah can reliably comment on her own behavior? Should she be brought into the discussion before any decisions are made? Why or why not? If so, how would you approach/include Sarah in the team's deliberations?

CHAPTER

8 Individual with Special Health Care Needs

Once again, Jamal is having an extended absence from school.

Characters: Jamal Warner, fourth grader
Captain Michael Warner, Jamal's father
Lawanda Barry, school nurse
Roberta Jeffry, homebound teacher
Linda Robbins, fourth-grade teacher

Flashpoint

It has been a hectic week and all Linda Roberts wants to do is pick up her child from latchkey and get home. She stops at her mailbox in the school office and notices a note has been placed there since lunchtime. The note is from Ms. Jeffry and simply states, "This crisis is over and Jamal is coming home from the hospital. He will be home for several weeks before returning to school. I'll be here first thing Monday morning to talk about what we need to do." Linda says out loud to no one in particular. "Oh no!"

Linda throws the note back in her mailbox and thinks to herself, "I never should have agreed to have Jamal in my class. When the special education teacher and the principal indicated he had sickle-cell anemia I had no idea what they were talking about. He is absent so often that it seems like I am always preparing special lessons for him. Fortunately, he is a strong reader so it has been easy to send home the language arts units. Captain Warner has been helpful in supporting Ms. Jeffry's teaching and assignments in math, but how in the world can Jamal take part in the culminating activity on American history?"

Reader Inquiry and Reflection
- Based on what you've read so far, what questions do you have about this situation?

- What additional information is needed?
- What information about the school, community, or family might be relevant to this case?

Background

Captain Michael Warner is a single father with two children, Jamal and his sister Tamika, a tenth grader at the High School. The children's mother died in an automobile accident three years ago, before Captain Warner was transferred to this area. Because of frequent promotions and transfers, the Warner family has moved four times since Jamal started kindergarten. Currently, the family lives in officers' housing at the base. Because of the rumors that the base will be closed, it is likely that the Warners will move again. Appropriate childcare has been a problem. Latchkey has provided some support, but unfortunately, Captain Warner believes that he relies on Tamika more than he should.

Jamal's sickle-cell anemia is a genetically inherited disease. Genetic screening is available and recommended prior to marriage to determine if one or both partners carry the recessive trait. Screening can also be done prenatally to determine if an unborn child has the gene mutation that carries sickle-cell anemia. Captain and Mrs. Warner did not avail themselves of either of these screenings. This gene mutation is most common in people of African American and Mediterranean descent. Sickle-cell anemia is a result of an abnormal genetic code that directs the body's production of hemoglobin. Jamal's red blood cells are not the typical round shape but are brittle and curved, shaped like a sickle. These abnormal cells are fragile and have shortened life spans. Situations like flying in an unpressurized airplane cabin or deep sea diving can trigger serious episodes that may require hospitalization or result in death if not treated. Sickle-cell crises have also been correlated with emotional stress and strenuous exercise.

Jamal has had a series of serious episodes that have resulted in his hospitalization and extended absences from school. During those times his class work is coordinated and monitored by Roberta Jeffry, the district's homebound teacher. To be successful this arrangement requires extensive collaboration between Ms. Jeffry and Linda Robbins. At times Jamal also takes pain medication, because the lack of red blood cells can cause circulation problems that result in severe pain. Jamal has a medication pump that permits him to receive medication on a constant basis. Mrs. Barry, the school nurse, has been very concerned with Jamal. She tries to come into the classroom when Jamal is there to monitor his pain levels.

Typical educational concerns for children with sickle-cell are increased fatigue, susceptibility to common contagious diseases (colds, flu, etc.), and, in some cases, a shortened life span. Peer relationships are also adversely affected by limited activities, frequent hospitalization, and extended school absences. At the last parent-teacher conference, Captain Warner shared his concern over the fact that Jamal doesn't seem to have any close friends. Another issue that can pose a problem for students with sickle-cell is school attendance policies. Some schools have a policy that states if a student misses more than six days a marking period they automatically fail that period regardless of the reason. DCSD is currently considering the implementation of such a policy. Jamal also must monitor his physical activity; he fatigues easily and cannot participate in contact sports. He also frequently has to use the bathroom, which can be disruptive to group activities.

Continuation and Closure

Jamal will be returning to school in a few weeks. Currently, in addition to routine coursework, Jamal's classmates are involved in a major project. The focus of fourth grade social studies at DCES is the study of American history. For the culminating activity the children are placed in three-person teams. Each team is assigned a period of history that they are to represent. After doing research from the textbook, the library, and local museums, the students come to school dressed in period costumes and give a brief report to the class about what they learned about the children of that era.

Questions/Activity/Task
- How can Linda Robbins and Roberta Jeffry coordinates efforts so that Jamal can participate in the culminating activity?
- How can communication between school, hospital, and family be facilitated?
- What can the family and school do to help Jamal establish and develop meaningful peer relationships?
- If DCSD adopts a strict attendance policy, should the implementation be different for Jamal and other students with similar problems? At what point, if any, can a student miss too much school to receive passing grades?

9 Individual with a Hearing Impairment

What is the best choice for dealing with Amy's hearing loss?

Characters: Amy Gonzalez, a 3-year-old child with an acquired moderate hearing loss

Dr. Maria Gonzalez and Jorge Gonzalez, parents

Lynn Cybulski, Fernald Center pre-primary specialist

Gloria Hernandez, speech-language pathologist

Alexa Horne, consultant for hearing impairments

Shirley Spires, teacher of school-based preschool and latchkey program

Dr. Harrison Moore, special education director

Flashpoint

Maria woke up thinking about the meeting she was attending this morning. She had rearranged her work schedule to accommodate the 11:00 meeting. Maria remembered thinking how lucky she was to have a flexible schedule, she briefly thought about all the other parents who were not as lucky. She was also glad Jorge was able to take an early lunch today and be at the meeting. As they got ready for the day, Maria and Jorge talked about what they wanted for Amy. They had heard many different opinions about Amy from both family and professionals since Amy's hearing loss. Some of the professionals they had encountered thought they should be teaching Amy sign language; others thought (including some relatives) that Amy should be learning Spanish and still others thought English was the language Amy should learn. Bilingualism was also recommended.

    Program decisions for Amy were also complicated. It was suggested that Amy should be in a program specifically for students with hearing impairments; others thought she should be in a program with typical children; yet others thought she should stay at home until she was older. It was all so confusing. Each professional had valid arguments to support his or her position. Maria and Jorge decided that they wanted Amy to be happy, and they wanted to find the best program for her. They also agreed, quietly to themselves, that if it was possible they wanted Amy to be her old self and the hearing loss to go away.

Although Maria had met most of the meeting participants as they evaluated Amy, it still made her nervous to think about all those people sitting around a table talking about Amy. She wondered what to expect from this, her first IEP meeting.

Reader Inquiry and Reflection

- Based on what you've read so far, what questions do you have about this situation?
- What additional information is needed?
- What information about the school, community, or family might be relevant to this case?

Background

The Gonzalezes met while both were undergraduate students at the Texas State University. Maria was in education and Jorge was studying hospital administration. After getting married and completing their advanced degrees, they applied for jobs throughout the country. They were very lucky to both get offered positions in Binet Lake. Maria is a professor at the community college and Jorge works in the hospital. They both have enjoyed the ten years they have lived in this community, and have been involved with local organizations and their church. However, they have missed the social contacts with their families and a larger Hispanic community. The Gonzalezes speak English at home, and both are also fluent in Spanish. They frequently visit Spanish-speaking relatives in Texas. They also maintain many of their cultural traditions in their home, including the annual celebration of Cinco de Mayo.

Amy is the youngest of the three Gonzalez children. The oldest, Hector, is in Mrs. Robbins' fourth-grade class and Terri (Theresa) is in second grade. Both children are doing well in school. Amy was born three years ago after a normal pregnancy and delivery. She obtained developmental milestones within expected levels including sitting, walking, babbling, and speaking single words in both Spanish and English. However, last year when she was 2, she developed an extremely high fever with the measles. She was hospitalized for several days. Fortunately, she recovered, but the experience resulted in a moderate to severe hearing loss in both ears. As a result, Amy can no longer hear speech sounds and relies heavily on visual cues to augment her residual hearing.

The nursing staffs at the hospital were just the beginning of the professional people Maria has worked with over the last six months. The hospital audiologist tested Amy's hearing after first teaching her how to respond to the tests. Finally, Amy learned to drop a block when she heard a sound. After determining the extent of loss, they made an ear mold and tried several different styles of hearing aids. An FM system with aids in both ears was recommended, because Amy was young. Maria and Jorge also met with a hospital speech pathologist and social worker who provided them information about the special education program offered through the regional educational support center. The hospital social worker urged them to contact Ms. Cybulski, the coordinator for early childhood special education services (for children 0 to 3 years of age) to learn about support services provided through the schools to young children.

Mrs. Cybulski explained about the family centered programs for children 0 to 3 years of age. She also described school-based programs for children 3 to 6. Services provided by the school included classroom programs and consultant services for the student based on an oral approach. Based on Maria's explanation of Amy's situation, it was decided to pursue additional assessment to gather information about Amy's learning styles, current language skills, and family concerns that could be used to develop a program for Amy. As a result, evaluations had been completed by school personnel who specialize in early childhood special education and as consultants for the hearing impaired. Maria had also been asked to sign a release of information so the information from the hospital could be considered in designing a program for Amy.

Maria mused that she was grateful for her background in education, because she understood the process and what the schools were attempting to do for Amy. Unfortunately, some of the relatives were not so understanding. They had already said some unkind things about Amy. One aunt had assumed that because Amy could no longer hear many things and was not talking, she was also stupid. The grandparents were insisting that Amy should be taught Spanish first so she could communicate with them on the visits. Maria sighed as she thought about the lack of understanding. Sometimes, even Hector and Terri became frustrated with Amy and some of their friends also did not understand.

Continuation and Closure

Maria snapped back to the present. Her immediate concern was the decisions she and her husband would be making today. After introductions, the meeting began with Ms. Hernandez's evaluation of Amy. She indicated that Amy's current level of understanding was about the same in English and Spanish. Ms. Hernandez also stated her opinion that with the hearing loss, it would be better if only one language was initially taught. She told the parents they could choose. Her experience suggested that the language of choice is a personal decision of the family and that she would support the Gonzalezes regardless of which language was chosen. Since she was also a fluent speaker of Spanish, she indicated she would assist in either language.

Ms. Horne completed her evaluation, and she suggested that Amy's instruction be based on an oral program. This means that Amy would receive direct instruction in speech reading and oral speech. This instruction would build on the skills and language she had learned prior to her illness. Mrs. Horne believed that with two years of hearing, Amy would be most successful with this approach. She added that with sign language, there is no written form and Amy would eventually need to learn a written language. There is also difficulty translating American Sign Language into Spanish. Maria thought she would really like Amy to learn Spanish.

The decision about educational programming was also important. Mrs. Gonzalez would like Amy to be with peers as much as possible. The preschool program run by Ms. Spires looked ideal. It was in the same school as Hector and Terri attended. However, Ms. Spires expressed doubts about being able to work with an FM system, check the batteries in the Amy's hearing aids, and make other accommodations to enable a child with hearing impairments to function. One concern Ms. Spires expressed was what if the fire alarm went off, how would Amy know what was happening? Mrs. Spires also did not know what to expect in terms of curriculum modifications. How could they accommodate Amy's lack of hearing and lack of language?

Questions/Activity/Task

- What are some of the issues that this family is facing? What resources or support would assist this family?
- Is support from the extended family and friends important? Why or why not? What are the issues from their perspective? What if anything could be done to increase their understanding of and support for the situation?
- What kinds of modifications would need to be made in the preschool environment to accommodate Amy? (Consider physical changes such as play areas, alarms, and signaling students.)

10 Individual with Visual Disability

When Frank Chesterfield transferred back to his neighborhood school, learning opportunities were presented to both students and teachers.

Characters: Frank Chesterfield, fourth grader

Kara and Bob Chesterfield, parents

Helen Arcadia, physical education teacher

Jerry Weiskoff, special education teacher

Flashpoint

"Of the million courses I took to become a PE teacher, couldn't one of them have covered the rules for Goal Ball!?!" Helen Arcadia's frustration increased as she unsuccessfully checked the indexes of the remaining textbooks in the box she resurrected from the basement. Yesterday, during lunchroom duty, she asked Frank to name his favorite sport, and his answer was "Goal Ball." Helen had never considered the possibility of having a blind student in her class. At this very moment she wasn't at all sure that she knew what to do. Frank Chesterfield's entrance into DCES was discussed at faculty orientation in August, but since Frank was in a self-contained classroom, Helen really had no contact with him. Frank had been attending the state residential school for the blind since he was 4 years old. This was his first year back in his neighborhood school. She was aware that Frank's IEP included the goal of partial inclusion into select classes, including PE, but that was months ago. Actually, most days she forgot Frank was there. "How convenient for all of us," Helen thought of the old stereotype, "making Frank invisible as well as blind."

When Jerry Weiskoff approached her with the idea, Helen told the special education teacher that she was willing to consider it, but was clueless as to the "what" and the "how." The whole notion was pretty scary—a blind kid in PE! What if he got hurt? Would she have to change her entire curriculum? What, if anything, could he do? How would the other fourth graders react? Jerry was very helpful, gave her the phone number of a friend who taught at the state residential school for the blind, and offered to arrange for both of them to visit the school. Jerry's collegial support was helpful; they were collaborating on ideas and sharing concerns. Even though it was several weeks before Frank Chesterfield would be attending PE with his fourth-grade classmates, there was a lot to do. "Goal Ball rules are the least of my worries," thought Helen.

Reader Inquiry and Reflection

- Based on what you've read so far, what questions do you have about this situation?
- What additional information is needed?
- What information about the school, community, or family might be relevant to this case?

Background

Frank Chesterfield was born two months premature with a dangerously low birth weight. The doctor advised his parents that although extended incubation and twenty-four hour intensive care were required for their son's survival, there were some risks associated with the recommended treatment regimen. One of those identified risks, retinopathy of prematurity (ROP), caused Frank's blindness. Frank's premature birth and subsequent treatment did not create any other deficits. His cognitive, affective, physical, and motor-skill development are comparable to other fourth graders.

DCSD through the Individualized Family Service Plan (IFSP) provided Kara and Bob Chesterfield with the services of a early intervention special education teacher while their son was an infant and toddler. The teacher worked with the Chesterfields in identifying local and state agencies and resources and also advised them on ways to enhance their son's development. Bob and Kara learned to purchase toys with tactile and auditory qualities that encouraged exploration and curiosity. Family field trips were also recommended. The Chesterfields took Frank everywhere with them—explaining sounds, touches and smells—helping him to build cognitive concepts through associations. When Frank was 4, Kara and Bob made the difficult decision to send their son to the state residential school for the blind, located several hours from their home in Binet Lake. The Chesterfields missed their son terribly but they knew that a residential facility would provide Frank a total adaptive educational experience, insuring that he would develop the skills necessary for success in the sighted world. Frank was now returning to his neighborhood school—a bright, capable, self-sufficient fourth grader with an almost unlimited future.

Continuation and Closure

The trip to the residential facility was a real eye-opener for both Jerry and Helen, and the long ride home provided an opportunity for them to process the experience. "Well, at least I learned how to play Goal Ball," Helen laughed. "Yeah, that PE program was most impressive," said Jerry, "I'll need to work with Frank on having realistic expectations for your class. Otherwise, he'll be very disappointed." In fact, Jerry wondered if Frank's entire experience at DCES had been disappointing; there was no way they could compete with the adapted environment of the residential school. However, it was very important for Frank to make the transition to succeeding in the sighted world, because that was his future. Helen and Jerry spent the rest of the trip discussing the specifics of Frank's inclusion in physical education. Fortunately, Frank had the sophisticated orientation and mobility skills necessary for even partial inclusion into any regular education classes. Helen's anxiety had diminished appreciably. According to the experts, Frank could only participate in certain activities in a traditional PE curriculum. So Helen and Jerry began to concentrate on what Frank could do rather than worry about what he couldn't do.

Sighted team sports were out of the question, but maybe by the end of the year Helen could plan a unit on Goal Ball, a team sport where Frank will be the resident expert. Until then, personal fitness activities such as jumping rope, aerobics, exercises, and relays using auditory signals would be the context for Frank's participation. The residential school's PE teacher showed Helen how to create an inexpensive auditory relay using highway cones with holes cut in them, transistor radios (to be placed inside the cones), and blindfolds for the sighted teams members. Sure sounded to Helen like the kind of game her fourth graders could get into! Actually, she planned on introducing all of her students to auditory team relays. Helen and Jerry did not want the entire focus of inclusion on Frank. The relays and (eventually) Goal Ball were worthwhile activities for all students and not just for the fourth graders.

Two issues still needed to be resolved. The first issue was how to structure Frank's PE time when he was unable to participate with the other students. Helen and Jerry both preferred that time to be spent on topics/activities related to physical education. For instance, Frank's social development would be enhanced if he understood something about various team sports. Not only could he not play sighted baseball, soccer, football or basketball, he had never seen any of the playing fields for those sports, and had no context for understanding the rules and purpose for the games. "What would be great," thought Helen, "would be to have raised, tactile playing fields that Frank could study, along with someone to explain the game and the rules written in Braille." "I'm sure I could order the rules in Braille, but how could I create or find tactile playing fields?" The second issue had to do with the best way to prepare the fourth graders for Frank's increasing participation in their classes. PE was first but mainstreaming in other classes would follow. Since this was his first year at DCES and since he had only been in a self-contained classroom, Frank and his blindness were still a curiosity and mystery to the other fourth graders.

Questions/Activity/Task

- What issues and information related to blindness should the fourth graders be exposed to prior to Frank's inclusion into the PE class?
- Whose responsibility is it to orient the fourth-grade students? What, if any, role should be played by Helen, Jerry and the fourth-grade teacher (Linda Robbins)?
- What strategies, activities, and experiences would you recommend for the orientation of the students to the issues identified in the first question?
- Any creative thoughts about how to produce tactile playing fields?

CHAPTER

11 Individual with Autistic Spectrum Disorder

What can the future possibly hold for a 14-year-old boy who does not speak or make eye contact with other human beings?

Characters: Blake Kwon, eighth grader

Lily and Master Sergeant Henry Kwon, parents

Lynn Cybulski, Fernald Center pre-primary specialist

Emma Siegel, language arts teacher

Shawn Quinn, special education resource teacher

Flashpoint

"OK, here we go," mused Emma Siegel, "stage two of the Blake Kwon experiment." Emma began to type, thinking that she was not at all sure this was going to work. But then, Blake had surprised teachers before. Even among students who have been diagnosed with autism, Blake was different. Still, it seemed pretty weird sending an e-mail message to a student seated no more than fifteen feet from her desk, not to mention a student who was totally nonverbal and did not make eye contact. Emma's message to Blake began to take form on her computer screen:

> Blake, this is Ms. Siegel. I'm going to ask you a question about today's story and I expect you to type me an answer right away. Why do you think Paul hesitated to join his friends when they invited him along on their train track adventure?

For all her doubts, Emma found herself rather excited about whether she would receive a response from Blake. "I certainly can't be more anxious than Shawn," thought Emma, "he's spent so much time with Blake trying to make sure he understood the process." Blake was very familiar with the hardware and software. In fact, word processing on a computer was Blake's only voice. However, the interactive reality of e-mail was an entirely new concept for Blake, which is why stage one of the experiment had been a several week orientation to interactive computing. Blake had been using a computer for his academic work since second grade. When he chose to, Blake would also word process his needs and wants. These latter expressions were decidedly one-way communication. Blake would write a statement, such as "I want to go for a walk," and would leave it on the screen until someone happened to come by and read it. It appeared that Blake did not expect or require a response to any thought he chose to express through word processing. "What a huge step it would be," Shawn told her this morning, "if we could get Blake to participate in purposeful, two-way communication. Think of the possibilities it would open up for that kid!"

A month ago Shawn came to Emma with this idea and enlisted her support. Shawn wanted to start slowly, in only one class; he chose Language Arts because it was Blake's strongest academic area and because Blake seemed more comfortable around Emma Siegel than any of his other teachers. Emma shuffled some papers on her desk, trying not to stare at the computer screen. She was pretty sure that Blake was oblivious to nonverbal cues but she didn't want to take any chances. All the while she was thinking, "C'mon, Blake! Let me hear that little 'beep' followed by the prompt, 'you have new mail'!!"

Reader Inquiry and Reflection

- Based on what you've read so far, what questions do you have about this situation?
- What additional information is needed?
- What information about the school, community, or family might be relevant to this case?

Background

Blake Edward Kwon's birth was joyfully greeted and celebrated by his immediate and extended family—the third child and only son born into a family with a long history of career military service. Though small and frail as an infant, he seemed physically healthy. However, compared to Henry and Lily's first two children, their baby boy did not seem as responsive to or interested in people or other stimuli. Henry's parents dismissed these concerns as simply being the difference between raising boys and girls. When Blake was not making noises or reaching for people and toys by his first birthday, the Kwons decided to share their concerns with the pediatrician on the army base in Germany. Blake was not at all verbal and he did not play. After what was an inadequate examination and assessment, the pediatrician concluded that Blake was retarded, and that the retardation was most likely the result of an intrauterine problem. The Kwons were devastated and Lily blamed herself for Blake's disability.

According to the Kwons, the best thing that ever happened to their family was when Henry was transferred to Kirk Army Base and Blake began receiving services from DCSD, the Fernald Center, and especially Lynn Cybulski. After an extensive and multifaceted assessment by the specialists at the Fernald Center, Blake's disability was diagnosed as autism rather than mental impairment. By age 2, Blake had developed persistent head-banging behavior in addition to his previous symptoms. DCSD provided a home-based program for Blake and his parents until he was 3 years old and eligible for the pre-primary impaired program at the Fernald Center. He remained in that program until age 6 and during that time Lynn Cybulski's astute observations and skillful interventions made a significant contribution to Blake's development.

Lynn Cybulski's initial case notes on Blake included the observation that he almost always carried around a stack of papers. Rather than dismiss this habit as simply another compulsive routine, Lynn decided to watch carefully what Blake did with the paper, i.e., did it serve a purpose? Blake collected and carried paper throughout the day and he defended and protected his stack. Lynn began to realize that Blake was not just collecting any piece of paper; he was only interested in paper that was printed with words. "Very interesting," Lynn thought, "this is purposeful behavior and could be the beginning of a relationship with words. This child may be cognitively intact, a high-functioning student with autism." Lynn made sure that she remained aware of Blake's collection of print and what he was doing with it. Within six months Blake would occasionally place his stack near Lynn absent any eye contact or communication. Lynn decided to interpret this behavior as a "read to me" request, even though it was virtually impossible to read to a kid who was in perpetual motion. Whenever Blake placed his stack near Lynn, she would immediately stop what she was doing and read the words printed on the top sheet of paper as fast as she could. This response seemed to satisfy Blake as he continued to "share" his stack with Lynn. By age 4, in addition to his ever-present stack, Blake also began to carry a blank scrap of paper and a marker. Not a pen, crayon, or pencil—they were aversive to him—only a marker. After a few days Blake started to make quick, fleeting marks on the blank paper and Lynn interpreted these as attempts to form pretend letters. With his collected stacks of print, his marker, blank scraps, and the trail of paper following him, Blake reminded Lynn of Pigpen in the "Peanuts" comic strip. The other thing worth noting was that Blake's head banging now only occurred when he was not involved with print. Within three months Blake was using his marker for inventive letter formation and finally to make recognizable consonants on his blank paper.

To challenge Blake further, Lynn created a large, felt communication board with a variety of felt word cards and icon cards. First, Blake placed his name card in front of an action word, i.e., "Blake eat." Lynn was elated because this was concrete evidence that Blake understood syntax; his cognition was at least average. After a while, Blake began leaving three- and four-word messages, and as with most 4-year-olds, some made sense and some did not. This was not active communication from Blake; he would leave the messages on the felt board for Lynn to find, and there was still no eye contact. A few months later, Blake abandoned the felt board and went solely to written communication. Lynn observed that Blake was moving his mouth while he was writing but whenever Lynn approached his "self-talk" would stop. Lynn needed to discover whether Blake was really verbalizing communication because this was the first indication that he could/would speak. Lynn placed several tape recorders set on "record" around the room, each containing extra long tapes. Through this creative detective work Lynn discovered that Blake was verbalizing, in fact, he was reading what he wrote even though he had not yet reached the age of 5. Blake was not cured; he still had the characteristics of a learner with autism and he would never communicate in the same form as his nonexceptional peers, but Blake was cognitively active and he could use language.

Because Blake's print collecting and writing behaviors were not very productive for developing social skills (he often snatched paper out of classmates' hands), Lynn decided to introduce Blake to word processing on a computer. Lynn set the computer in a part of the room Blake frequented, turned it on, pulled up a word processing page, told Blake it was "his" and put his name on it, and waited to see what would happen. Blake took to the computer as though he had been waiting for it. He used the computer consistently but not compulsively. He still carried his "piles" everywhere but he no longer grabbed paper away from his peers. Lynn gave Blake verbal responses to his word-processed messages and slowly the circle of communication began to expand. By the time he turned 6, Blake would tolerate his peers responding verbally to items they read on Blake's computer screen. The computer became Blake's link to the world and the Kwons purchased a computer for Blake to use at home. Blake left the Fernald Center prior to his seventh birthday and beginning in second grade he spent the majority of his school day in a regular classroom. Blake has a laptop computer that he takes to all his classes. He excels in traditional language-based courses such as social studies and language arts. Blake is much weaker academically in the arts and mathematics and his motor skills are not very good. Blake still does not communicate verbally and avoids eye contact.

Continuation and Closure

"Beep," the computer alerted and Emma Siegel broke into a huge grin as she read, "You have new mail." Emma accessed Blake's response and read; "I think Paul hesitated because he knew that these particular friends were planning something illegal." Emma thought "Yes, Blake!!!" but she responded with, "Thank you, Blake.

Your answer shows insight into Paul's thoughts and state laws." Emma's head was swimming with ideas as she headed down to the resource room to tell Shawn the good news. Luckily, they had the same prep period so they could celebrate Blake's accomplishment and think about what should happen next. "What does this mean?" Emma wondered, "Could we use e-mail for Blake to participate in class discussions? Should we find him some e-mail pen pals? How about the internet? Wow! Are the possibilities really this endless?"

Questions/Activity/Task

- Since Blake's initial experience with interactive computing was successful, what should Shawn and Emma plan as a follow-up in Language Arts? At what point, if ever, should interactive computing with Blake be extended to other teachers and classes? Which class or classes should be considered and why?

- Would you recommend that the process of interactive computing be introduced at home? Why or why not? If so, when and how?

- In a few months Shawn Quinn will be meeting with the high school special and regular education teachers and counselors to begin discussing educational and possibly career planning options for Blake Kwon. What do you think the future holds for Blake? What kind of things do you think should be considered for Blake's ninth grade IEP and transition plan?

- What activities and community resources might assist Blake in developing more age-appropriate social skills?

CHAPTER

12 Individual with a Traumatic Brain Injury

Irina is very excited about attending music class for the first time. Unfortunately, no one told Mr. Lewis.

Characters: Irina Kochenka, a seventh grade student

Donna Bray, assistant principal

Lawanda Barry, school nurse

Roberta Jeffry, homebound teacher

Robert Lewis, general music teacher/chorus director

Mark Milligan, special education teacher consultant

Flashpoint

Ms. Bray, the assistant principal at the middle school, smiled to herself as she returned to school from an all-morning meeting with the superintendent. The first seven weeks of the fall semester were almost over and the school was settling down to a comfortable routine. The sixth graders seemed to understand the system and were confidently changing classes, negotiating the halls, surviving lunch, and handling the locks and lockers. As she had hoped, the seventh and eighth graders seemed to be providing stability and leadership. It had been a good school start this year.

She could not understand why the Kochenka family had called three times this morning. The Kochenka's daughter, Irina, was a student certified for special education support, and the secretary indicated that Mrs. Kochenka sounded very distressed. In fact, she was now waiting in the office and would want to meet as soon as Ms. Bray entered the school. Her other duties would need to wait a while. Ms. Bray mused, "I guess I'm glad I called to check on things before returning to the building."

As they entered Ms. Bray's office, Mrs. Kochenka looked at Ms. Bray and said, "What are we going to do about music? Irina is scheduled to begin general music next week and we do not have a plan." Then Ms. Bray remembered that at the IEPT meeting last spring it was determined that Irina would participate in electives this year, but the specifics of how that would be accomplished would happen as needed. It certainly was needed now. Ms. Bray also wondered if anyone had told Mr. Lewis that Irina would be in his class for the next marking period.

Reader Inquiry and Reflection

- Based on what you've read so far, what questions do you have about this situation
- What additional information is needed?
- What information about the school, community, or family might be relevant to this case?

Background

The inclusion program for the students in special education seemed to be working. Even though this was the first year that Ms. Bray was responsible for the inclusion program at the middle school, she was pleased with how smoothly things were running. The general and special educators had formed several teams and co-taught sections of academic classes. In addition, Mark Milligan, the building-based teacher consultant, was available to assist with students who were "certified" for special education services. There also was a cross-categorical resource room where students from all special education categories spent up to half of the day receiving services specific to their needs. Lawanda Barry, the school nurse, helps coordinate physical and occupational therapy appointments for those students receiving such services. Ms. Barry also monitors and distributes medication to students as needed. The parents, teachers, and students seemed to find the arrangement workable. The middle school had students with learning disabilities, emotional impairments, speech and language impairments, educable mental impairments, hearing impairments, and physical impairments.

Irina Kochenka first enrolled in the DCMS last year as a sixth grader. Her parents were hard-working Russian immigrants who are successful farmers. The family is bilingual and Irina speaks both Russian and English. As a sixth grader, Irina attended a self-contained classroom for students with physical impairments or special health care needs (PI). She was eligible for this service because had been in an automobile accident that resulted in a traumatic brain injury (TBI). The family continues to experience high medical costs resulting from Irina's accident. As self-employed farmers, they do not have comprehensive medical insurance.

In Irina's case the TBI left her with moderate fine and gross motor difficulties (impaired function to both arms and legs) with speech difficulties. Transportation to and from school is provided in a bus with a lift. For mobility, Irina uses a walker on wheels to move from place to place. The walker is adjustable to Irina's height and is able to provide some stability as she walks. Because she uses a walker, she is released from class early, but she also fatigues easily. Some experts have suggested that she uses ten times as much energy as a typical person for most activities. Irina also has difficulty controlling her arm and hand movements. She has learned to word process using one finger and uses some one-word voice commands to facilitate the process. However, writing is still a slow and laborious process for her. Her speech is also slow and labored, although she can be understood in both English and Russian. She does have an electronic note taker that she uses in her academic classes and it has a modified keyboard that makes it easier for her to input data. The notes can be downloaded into a desktop computer for editing.

General learning characteristics of Irina that impact school performance include a labored and irregular speech and language, slow processing of questions, frequent absenteeism due to illness and doctors' appointments, and limited memory for language. Irina currently has modified exams, usually allowing longer time to complete them or shorter exams. Most assignments are also modified to take advantage of her computer knowledge or shortened to accommodate the extraordinary amount of time and energy it takes her to complete them. Roberta Jeffry, the homebound teacher, assists Irina when her health requires extended absences from school. Ms. Jeffry facilitates communication between school, family, doctor, and Irina. She also coordinates assignments from Irina's teachers and helps Irina stay current with class content. Because of these homebound services, Irina's extended absences have not resulted in retention or poor grades.

Irina continues to demonstrate gifted abilities in the math area. She is doing well in seventh grade math and the counselors are talking about including her name in the list of students eligible for the math enrichment program. Her current math teacher has modified her requirements because of the length of time it takes Irina to complete a problem. Usually she has shortened assignments or only has to write an answer to a problem, not copy the entire problem. She also is able to use her computer to complete her math assignments, because it is a necessary tool for her, much like an HI student uses a hearing aid, although initially, the math teacher thought it would be unfair to the other students if Irina used an electronic device.

Irina's current educational program, as designated on the IEP, has her attending the resource room for English, Social Studies, and Science. She is in a co-taught math class and has adapted physical education. She also receives speech and physical therapy during the school day and beginning next week will start music class. Irina's speech difficulties interfere with singing and she has not learned to read music. However, she likes music and is very much looking forward to the class. Mrs. Kochenka indicated that Irina had talked about music all summer and a chance to be with her friends in a "cool" class.

The general music class at the seventh grade level includes some musical history and theory, but the emphasis is on singing. The class works together and presents a short vocal music program at the end of the eight weeks.

Continuation and Closure

As Ms. Bray and Mrs. Kochenka talked, it became clear that a plan was going to have to be designed within the next week. Irina was going to go to music class.

Questions/Activity/Task

- Who should inform Mr. Lewis about his new student, Irina, and when should Mr. Lewis be told about her?
- What are the first two or three things you would consider in devising a plan for Irina in her music class? (Think about what kinds of modifications would need to be made in terms of personnel, curriculum, and teaching strategies. Be sensitive to her need for extra time and her energy level.)
- How could the technology Irina uses be able to assist her in music class?
- What are some options Mr. Lewis could use to grade Irina?

CHAPTER

13 Individual with Severe Multiple Impairments

Tamika has been very successful in a center-based program for students with multiple impairments. Is now the time for her to return to her neighborhood school?

Characters: Tamika Collins 9-year-old student (fourth-grade age level)

Mrs. Collins, Tamika's mother

Kenyatta (10 years) and Caleb (7 years) Collins, Tamika's siblings

Jerry Weiskoff, special education teacher

Linda Robbins, fourth-grade teacher

Edna Ewell, principal

Mrs. Montgomery, concerned parent of a fourth-grade student (Susan) and neighbor of the Collins.

Flashpoint

The telephone call from Mrs. Montgomery had caught Ms. Ewell by surprise. Mrs. Montgomery is active in the school, often volunteering in her children's classes and assisting with the annual book sale. She is generally very supportive of the school and one of its biggest boosters. Today, she was very concerned that the academic standards in the school and the fourth grade in particular were being compromised by the inclusion of so many students with disabilities. Mrs. Montgomery went on to say that in Susan's class she knew that there was the boy who couldn't see, a boy in a wheelchair, maybe others, and now Tamika, her neighbor's child, may be coming. It was just too much. Mrs. Montgomery was concerned that everyone was looking out for the children with disabilities, but no one was concerned about what happened to the typical children, including her daughter.

Ms. Ewell listened attentively and tried to reassure Mrs. Montgomery that the academic standards were not being compromised and it was her job as principal to assure that this wouldn't happen. Mrs. Montgomery seemed temporarily satisfied but said she was not at all sure about this and would continue to think about it. When she hung up the telephone, Ms. Ewell thought how fast news traveled around the school and that some of her teachers had the same questions that Mrs. Montgomery raised. It was time to find out more about Tamika and if Mrs. Montgomery's information was correct.

Reader Inquiry and Reflection

- Based on what you've read so far, what questions do you have about this situation?
- What additional information is needed?
- What information about the school, community, or family might be relevant to this case?

Background

Tamika Collins is a 10-year old girl. Currently she attends the Fernald Center. She is eligible for special education services as a child with multiple impairments. According to her pediatrician, she was diagnosed with spastic cerebral palsy at birth. As a result the muscles in her arms and legs are very tight and difficult for her to control their movement. As a toddler she was also diagnosed with developmental delays. Three years ago, at the time of her last comprehensive reevaluation, she had an IQ score between 50–54 with delays also noted in speech, language, and adaptive behaviors. As a result she also was labeled as a child with moderate mental impairments, and thus was a child with multiple impairments.

Tamika arrives at the Fernald Center on the bus with the lift. She does need help getting on and off the bus. The teacher aide assigned to her classroom usually provides this service. Her teacher at the Fernald Center indicates that Tamika can move around a little on the floor by a scooting system, but most of the time uses a wheelchair to move around her classroom and the Center. She has developed some arm control and writes using an adaptive writing tool. Typically, this is a marker with a special grip that makes it easier for her to hold. She can print her name, if the paper is stable. Often it is taped to the top of her chair tray for stability. She is beginning to talk, but currently says only single words. It is a slow and laborious process for Tamika to coordinate the breathing, muscle control, and thoughts required to speak. The listener needs to be patient and wait for Tamika to respond. She does follow conversation and will attempt to take turns. Tamika is following a specialized curriculum that emphasizes self-care skills (including feeding and dressing), communication, basic academics, social skills, and motor skill development. Tamika also receives specialized support from the occupational therapist, physical therapist, and speech-language pathologist. The teachers and staff at the Fernald Center are very proud of Tamika. They believe she has made significant progress for the seven years she has been attending classes there.

Mrs. Collins has also been pleased by Tamika's progress in academic and language areas. Tamika can even almost say, "I love you" to her mother. However, she is concerned that Tamika is not comfortable with other children her age. Mrs. Collins would like to see more emphasis on developing social skills. She thinks that best way to do this is have Tamika interact more often with the children in the neighborhood she already knows and who can model appropriate social skills. One way to facilitate this is to have Tamika attend the neighborhood school where her other children, Kenyatta and Caleb, go to school. Additionally, she thinks it would be easier for the family to have all the children on the same schedule with the same vacations, bus schedule, conference days, etc. Mrs. Collins feels very strongly about this and was casually talking to her neighbor, Mrs. Montgomery, about how exciting it would be if all her children could go to school together. Mrs. Collins indicated that it was a dream of hers to have Tamika go to school just like the other kids. It was this conversation that prompted Mrs. Montgomery's telephone call to Ms. Ewell.

Continuation and Closure

Ms. Ewell thought about the possibility of Tamika's attending her school. There were many questions about including a child with the serious physical and cognitive delays that Tamika presented. There were at least several teachers in the school who had voiced that idea that if they wanted to teach special education students they would have picked that major in school. Could those teachers adequately prepare their students to accept Tamika in the school? There was also the question of curriculum. Certainly Tamika could not even begin to achieve the fourth-grade goals. Could anything be gained by having her sit in the classroom? This was the year the SWAT (Statewide Achievements Test) would be given. Tamika certainly wouldn't have to take that, would she? Had Mrs. Collins even thought about that? Did the staff at the Fernald Center really think that the curriculum they had developed for students with multiple disabilities could be implemented in her school? What about Mrs. Robbins? She already had three students with special needs in her class, including Gemma. If possible, Mrs. Collins wanted Tamika in the fourth grade, or perhaps she was thinking about the self-contained classroom, which would be Mr. Weiskoff. The more Ms. Ewell thought about this, the more questions she had, including if it was possible to maintain high academic standards and still include all children in her school. Is it likely that more parents will have concerns about Tamika? Also, rumors often spread quickly and she will need to have some information to share with the parents and her staff. She picked up the telephone and made a call.

Questions/Activity/Task

- Who do you think Edna Ewell should be calling? What other initial steps and information gathering would you recommend?
- Based on the information provided, what is the least restrictive environment for Tamika? What service delivery option would best meet her needs?
- What recommendation would you make for helping Tamika increase her level of social skills?
- If Tamika is assigned to a general education classroom for part of the day, how can Edna Ewell adequately prepare the teachers, parents, and other students?
- Since Mrs. Robbins has three other students with special learning needs, should this be part of the decision? Can she meet the needs of Tamika and her other typical and exceptional students?
- How can Mr. Weiskoff facilitate the inclusion process?

14 Individual Educational Planning Team (IEPT)

Carlos has been struggling with some of his academic subjects for the last two years. His behavior is starting to become a problem in school, but does the IEPT have sufficient data to determine whether he is eligible for special education support?

Characters: Carlos Rivera, tenth-grade student

Mr. and Mrs. Rivera, Carlos's parents

James Campbell, principal

Justine Bai, tenth-grade English teacher

Daryl Cooper, tenth-grade math teacher

Coach John Davis, physical education teacher

Darlene Hilmann, school nurse

Eliot Santi, special education teacher

Marsha Matchwick, school psychologist

Gloria Antonelli, speech-language pathologist

Flashpoint

Mr. Campbell was arranging chairs around the conference table in preparation for the upcoming IEPT. In a few minutes the Riveras, their son Carlos, two of the teachers, and several support staff would be arriving for the IEPT on Carlos. Mr. Campbell didn't think all of Carlos's teachers would attend the IEPT meeting, because they weren't all able or willing to stay after school for the meeting. He trusted that Ms. Matchwick and Mr. Santi had scheduled this meeting so at least one of the general education staff would be present. Mr. Campbell began to think about Carlos.

Recently, he had gotten to know Carlos better, primarily because he had been sent to the office for discipline several times within the last several months. It was nothing serious, smart aleck comments, refusal to turn in work, and skipping class for an extended lunch. However, there was a concern that a pattern was forming that was not supportive of Carlos's continued education and there were concerns that he might drop out of school when he reached his sixteenth birthday. This upcoming IEPT may just develop a plan that would meet Carlos's needs. He certainly hoped it would have an impact on Carlos.

Reader Inquiry and Reflection

- Based on what you've read so far, what questions do you have about this situation?
- What additional information is needed?
- What information about the school, community, of family might be relevant to this case?

Background

Carlos was the oldest of three children in the Rivera family. All of the children were born in this country, although Mr. and Mrs. Rivera immigrated as children. Spanish is spoken occasionally in the home when communicating with relatives. Mrs. Rivera had been an involved parent for each of the children. She was a room mother for her daughter in elementary school and a volunteer at the middle school library where her other daughter attended school. She had done similar kinds of things when Carlos was younger, but he didn't want her at the high school. She respected his wishes and did not volunteer on a regular basis, but she had always been available for conferences. Mr. Rivera was a long distance truck driver. As a result, he was frequently away from home for days at a time. When he was home, he was less interested in school activities. However, he would attend the kids' sporting events and concerts. He used to play ball with Carlos, but again Carlos is no longer interested in spending as much time with his family.

A review of the school records indicates an inconsistent pattern. In early elementary school Carlos's report card showed mostly Bs with notes about his leadership skills and his ability to solve problems and think creatively. In middle school his grades in English, math, and social studies began to slip. There were notes about not turning in written assignments and homework, but he contributed important ideas in class discussions. There were also a few notes of behavior problems, primarily on the playground where he seemed to lead a group of boys to cause minor problems. For example, at lunch one day, four eighth graders left the school grounds and walked to the neighborhood convenience store for some snacks. The students were caught returning to school for last hour, but they had broken several rules by leaving the grounds and skipping classes. The classes Carlos tended to skip were English and Social Studies. His teachers in the middle school expressed the opinion that perhaps Carlos' behaviors and school performance could be explained by a learning disability in the written language area, but his parents refused to sign permission for the evaluation. The teachers had attempted to make modifications and allow Carlos to complete more hands-on projects and take some oral tests. This resulted in minor improvements in his grades and he was sufficiently successful to be passed into the high school.

His ninth grade year was not productive. Carlos seemed to try at the beginning of the year, but as the demands increased he had more difficulty. Carlos still seemed to understand the work, but was refusing to turn in homework or many written assignments. The assignments he did turn in tended to be three or four short sentences, full or errors, and almost illegible. Carlos managed to barely pass each of his classes and had enough credits to be considered a sophomore. However, again this year the same problems were evident and there was a real possibility that Carlos would not earn sufficient credits to move the eleventh grade. He still seemed to be a leader among his friends, but his leadership skills were not always used in ways that the school found acceptable. His teachers, particularly Ms. Bai, the English teacher, were concerned about him. She described Carlos as a likable young man who has more information than he is sharing with us. It was Ms. Bai who convinced Mrs. Rivera that Carlos should be evaluated to assess his learning style and the possibility he had a learning disability. Mrs. Rivera trusted Ms. Bai, thought she was a good teacher, and was truly concerned about Carlos's future.

Mrs. Rivera was aware of the seriousness of Carlos's problem. She had been to conferences over the last two years and heard about the problems from his teachers. She saw her son struggle. She knew that Carlos would often look at his homework, then decide there was too much and quit. Other times, he would spend an hour trying to write one or two sentences and quit in frustration as he watched his sister write a full page in a few minutes. When the school personnel again asked for permission to evaluate Carlos, she had reluctantly given her permission. Her husband did not believe that Carlos had any problems. When he was home, he didn't see Carlos doing any homework; he always seemed to be off with his friends. He believed that Carlos was just acting like a young man and the school needed to be stricter.

Mrs. Rivera agreed to the evaluation and an assessment-planning meeting was held. At that time the assessment team including the school psychologist, the special education teacher, Ms. Bai, Mrs. Rivera, and Mr. Campbell decided the following evaluations should be completed:

A psychological evaluation to determine current skill levels and aptitude

A speech and language evaluation to determine if second language issues were a concern

A physical because Mrs. Rivera reported Carlos had seasonal allergies

Current evaluations by his teachers, progress and concerns in each of his classes

A social work assessment of current socioemotional development and interview Carlos about his likes and dislikes

The special education teacher consultant would also complete a more in-depth look at the areas of weakness identified by the teachers and school psychologist and attempt to identify teaching strategies that would be appropriate.

Continuation and Closure

It took about two months, but the testing was finally completed. The results were summarized on the Multi-Disciplinary Evaluation form that Mr. Campbell had brought in to the conference room for the meeting. The official reports would be attached to the IEP at the end of the meeting with the parents receiving a copy of all the materials. Carlos, his parents, the support staff, and teachers had all arrived and the IEPT meeting was going to start. Mr. Campbell chaired the meeting and began with introductions. Mrs. Rivera knew everyone, but Mr. Rivera seldom attended parent-teacher meetings and did not know everyone at the IEPT meeting. After introductions, each member gave his or her report and the Riveras expressed their perspective as summarized below:

The report summaries are:

- *English teacher*—Ms. Bai reported that in her class, Carlos would participate in discussion but would seldom turn in written work. What he did turn in was not acceptable, and he would not redo it. She routinely held afterschool help sessions, but Carlos only attended once. When he found out he still had to write, he never came back. She also indicated that at times he was defiant in classroom. He currently is failing English.
- *Math teacher*—Mr. Cooper reported that Carlos was doing about C– work in his class. He would do the assignments that required Carlos just to write answers, but if he had to show his work or do more comprehensive writing, the assignments did not get done. Carlos would likely be getting a better grade if he completed more assignments; he seems to understand that math process. When class time was available for completing problems, Carlos would become a class wit and not concentrate on completing his work. Several of the students would follow his lead if given a chance. "He seems like a nice kid."

- *Physical education*—Carlos is getting an A in gym,
- *Science*—Carlos is getting a D in Science. He will not turn in written assignments, but does well on his lab when his partner does the writing. The multiple-choice part of the exams is carrying his test scores. He cannot write a coherent paragraph.
- *Government*—Carlos participates in class discussions, but has missed several class periods. His chapter exams are inconsistent. He does well on some, but poorly on others. "He seemed to enjoy the simulation of the federal government we did at the beginning of the semester, but his participation has declined since that time. He is currently getting a D–."
- *Speech-language pathologist*—Carlos's primary language is English, he is a competent speaker of English, and struggles with Spanish. It is not believed that this would hinder his understanding or ability to complete school assignments in English.
- *School nurse*—Mrs. Hillman indicated that a report was received from Carlos's physician. The report indicated that while Carlos has some mild allergies, they are controllable by over-the-counter medication. This may lead to some drowsiness, but would likely not interfere with his ability to learn. He does not have asthma or serious allergic reactions. The doctor further reports that Carlos is healthy and is appropriate height and weight for his age, his immunizations are up-to-date, and no other health problems are noted.
- *School psychologist*—Marcia Matchwick completed her evaluation and found that on the Wechsler Intelligence Scale for Children-III, Carlos had a full-scale score in the average range (FSIQ 105). However, he had difficulty completing the Coding subtest, which required the ability to rapidly write symbol code when matched to specific numbers. An achievement screening was completed using the Wechsler Individual Achievement test. Again scores were in the average range in math and reading. However, written expression scores were well below average (standard score 75). Ms. Matchwick also noted in her report that Carlos would become noticeably agitated when asked to write responses. He was more comfortable and gave more complete answers when asked to respond verbally.
- *Special education teacher*—Mr. Santi tested Carlos's written language more closely. He found that Carlos struggled with production—that is, he had difficulty translating his ideas into written form. His letter formation was slow and laborious. He would become frustrated attempting to get words on paper and would frequently erase, draw lines through words, and just quit. His scores reflected below average abilities in written language.

The testing was now completed and the results were going to be shared with Carlos and the Riveras at the meeting that would start in a few minutes.

Carlos had seemed to be on "good behavior" all day. Perhaps he was a little nervous or apprehensive about the upcoming meeting, especially since he had agreed to attend.

- *Mr. Rivera*—"I think Carlos is a smart boy and can do his work, he just doesn't want to. He would rather be hanging out with his friends and besides it's not 'cool' to be a student. He wants to drive a truck like me and doesn't need school. When I'm on the road, Carlos is the responsible 'man of the house' and that keeps him busy. He is responsible."

- *Mrs. Rivera*—Mrs. Rivera indicated that Carlos could be a little difficult to manage when his dad is out of town. He thinks he doesn't always have to listen to her and will skip his homework. She also noticed that he has allergies and when his eyes itch and he is sneezing, he doesn't have as much energy to complete his schoolwork. She did state that other times Carlos will struggle for hours to write a few sentences before he stomps out of the house frustrated.

Questions/Activites/Tasks

- How do you think Carlos feels participating in this discussion? What can the other participants do to increase Carlos's comfort. Should Carlos be interviewed as part of the proceedings? Why or why not?

- Should additional assessments be conducted? Why or why not?

- Based on the information available, do you think Carlos is eligible for special education services? Why or why not? If yes, in what category(s) of eligibility would you place Carlos? What evidence supports this decision?

- Taking into account your decision regarding eligibility, what curricular and behavioral strategies and modifications would you recommend for Carlos?

- Considering Carlos's age, should vocational planning and/ or placement be part of Carlos's IEP? What would be your recommendation as to the form this should take?